THE MARTIAL
SPIRIT an introduction to the
origin, philosophy, and psychology
of the martial arts

HERMAN KAUZ

Photographs by Tetsu Okuhara

The Overlook Press
Woodstock, New York

First published in 1977 by
The Overlook Press
Lewis Hollow Road
Woodstock, New York 12498
Copyright © 1977 by Herman Kauz
Photographs Copyright ©1977 Tetsu Okuhara
Library of Congress Catalog Card Number: 77-77808
ISBN: 0-87951-067-6

Illustrations

The photographs have been provided to help give those readers unfamiliar with martial arts some idea of the look and feel of the best known of these disciplines. The differences between the various arts written about also become more apparent when they appear visually. Still another reason for presenting the illustrations is the hope that the viewer will sense the mental and psychological aspects of this training.

Order of Photographs

CONTENTS

8

FOREWORD

As A STUDENT of Asian martial arts for almost 30 years and a teacher for 25, my thinking about the function and value of studying these disciplines has undergone a number of changes. My ideas were, naturally, strongly tied to my experiences in training. In retrospect, my meanderings in the martial arts appear to have followed a sequential pattern of development. This sequence might be acceptable in terms of the idea that all roads eventually lead to the same end. Yet, I know that the pattern I will describe is something of an illusion. It is probably formed by the rational mind's tendency to select certain memories of events from among many in the past and to arrange them in a way that seems logical and coherent.

I began to study judo in Hawaii soon after World War II. I had done some wrestling prior to this, but when an opportunity to begin judo training afforded itself I took it. It became my major interest. I soon found, however, that my preconceptions about judo as the ultimate in self-defense were wrong. The judo I was learning was sport judo and not the kind of jujitsu and karate combination my reading had led me to expect. Nevertheless, I continued to practice and gradually found myself being caught up in this training. The competitive aspect of judo also attracted me. In addition, I slowly became aware of and interested in a Japanese way of doing things.

After studying judo for eight years and teaching it for about four, I went to Japan (1956-1958) to continue my training. To practice judo in Japan had been my intention for a number of years, because judo originated there and the level of the art was reputed to be higher there than anywhere else. While in Japan, I became interested in karate and began to study that art daily for about two years. Karate training differed slightly from that encountered in judo in that more of the training consisted of individual practice. Moreover, at that time, competition in karate was not as strongly emphasized as it was in judo.

In 1958, I returned to New York and resumed teaching judo. Because of the rising interest in karate, I taught this as well. During this period I practiced kendo briefly and continued studying aikido with a friend who was a teacher of that discipline. I had studied aikido for a short time in both Hawaii and Japan.

As the years passed, my approach to the study and teaching of martial arts continued to change. My earlier emphasis on self-defense and competition began to move more in the direction of training as a preparation for, or an aid in, living as fully and completely as possible. As I reflected on the changes my study of martial arts had made in me, I realized that my training had been something more than the surface, body-strengthening, skill-producing kind. I became aware that an inner development was also intended and had occurred. The beginning of an interest in Zen also contributed to this change in my outlook.

In 1963, I decided to go to Japan once again to study Zen and to continue my training in judo and karate. I stayed for about two years and then returned to New York where I began a study of tai chi chuan. Tai chi attracted me strongly because it combined the mental and physical aspects of martial arts training in the proportions I had come to feel were right for me. Presently, almost all my efforts are devoted to practicing and teaching tai chi.

A word may be in order about what this book contains and what it attempts to emphasize. It was not my intention to discuss all of the martial arts presently taught in the United States. I have confined myself only to those arts that are best known and most easily available and have made no effort to exhaustively delineate the technical aspects even of those. Where I have, in a limited sense, discussed technical aspects, the martial art in question is one of which I have had personal experience.

Moreover, the history of the various martial arts has not been included. One reason for this decision is that history sometimes seems an attempt to select certain occurrences from among many in the past and to assign these significance in accord with present thinking. At the least, the relative importance of certain happenings changes as the thinking of the historian changes. However, these distortions aside, as we go further into the past of martial arts, we are faced with a scarcity of trustworthy information on which to base a meaningful history. In some systems, martial arts techniques and methods were kept secret and passed on from master to student without the knowledge of outsiders. Sometimes the origins of a martial art were intentionally shrouded in mystery by those passing on traditions by word of mouth. In such cases, there may have been an attempt to link the art with supernatural elements or to some philosophical or religious principle the culture valued.

In broad terms, if we accept the theories of anthropological study concerning the impact of major thought currents in a culture on everything done in that culture, it seems logical to expect the teachers of martial arts to have absorbed elements of the overriding ideas of their time. Thus, Taoism, Confucianism and Buddhism, in those countries where these philosophical systems held sway, cannot but have exerted a good deal of influence on the martial arts practiced there. But the nature and extent of changes, or whether a martial art came into existence because of the philosophical climate, seems open to speculation.

Again, broadly speaking, the martial arts that we know today are derived from combat forms. But they have also been used, even in the distant past, as physical and mental training. Whatever their origins, the influences that shaped them or even past employment, we must concern ourselves with what these arts can do for us now. In our time, fighting as it was known earlier is generally no longer done or required. However, the martial arts have lost none of their potential for physical and mental development. This book is especially concerned with the mental training which can be found in all the martial arts.

The ideas I hold about the direction in which martial arts training should go are not shared by all who practice or teach these arts. Among those who would generally agree with my point of view, a much smaller number would place primary emphasis upon inner development. Nevertheless, my experience in studying and teaching martial arts over a fairly long period of time has gradually brought me to my present view. My hope in writing this book is that I might turn others in a direction I have found very helpful for living.

12

CHAPTER I

Introduction

IN THE LAST twenty years, the United States—and the entire Western world, for that matter—has seen a tremendous growth in Asian martial arts. Before World War II, such fighting systems as judo, jujitsu and karate were systematically studied by very few Occidentals. In the United States, communities with a large Asian population usually had schools which taught martial arts, but they were often closed to outsiders. A few books were available on the subject and sometimes magazine advertisements appeared which made extravagant claims for an Asian fighting system. Readers were told that in a few easy lessons, or by reading a book, they would be able to defend themselves against any attack. Anyone who tried to learn a fighting system in this way usually became frustrated and disappointed, because these arts cannot be learned from a book. However, this condition was soon to change. With the stationing of hundreds of thousands of American troops in Japan after 1945 and in Korea in the 1950s, many soldiers began to study Asian martial arts seriously. Some learned enough to begin teaching after they returned home. Interest in the martial arts grew as places to practice increased and as those who had spent some time studying began to show some degree of expertise.

Not surprisingly, the most widespread of the Asian fighting systems in this country have been the judo and karate of Japan and Korea. The personal contact established between American soldiers and their teachers sometimes resulted in an Asian teacher being invited to teach here. This situation contributed to the growth in the number of schools teaching a particular Japanese or Korean martial art. In recent years, American cities with a Chinatown have seen a large influx of Chinese. Among them have been teachers of various Chinese boxing systems (usually called kung fu). Some of these Chinese systems, such as shaolin chuan and tai chi chuan, are now beginning to vie for popularity with the more established Asian systems.

To attract students, proprietors of martial arts schools in the United States have stressed the self-defense aspects of these arts, capitalizing on people's fear of street crime. Some entrepreneurs in this field have staged martial arts contests and shows. These usually conclude when all except one of the competitors have been eliminated and he is crowned the grand champion of a particular style for a short period of time. These shows also feature demonstrations concerned with the ability of the human body, unaided by tools, to generate the kind of power that can crack ice, shatter bricks and split wood.

Japanese and Chinese moviemakers have introduced Asian martial arts to a wide audience in the West. The Japanese films are sometimes works of art that make some moving or important comment on the human condition. The fighting seen in these films is usually done by warriors, or *samurai,* and ranges from unarmed combat to the use of sword and spear. These *samurai* are portrayed as living by a certain warrior's code, a code which their martial arts training helped to instill. By contrast, the Chinese martial arts movies usually seen by American audiences seem merely vehicles to display the talents of the featured martial artist. The best known of such films presented the late Bruce Lee as the "good guy" in numerous encounters with "bad guys" whom he overcomes with the skillful use of fists and feet. The training that produced Lee's skill and the use of this training to achieve results that go beyond the development of skill are not stressed.

In addition to seeing movies that display Asian fighting skills, television viewers could, in the early seventies, watch a weekly program which dealt with the exploits in the old West of a Chinese monk trained in martial arts. On this program, flashbacks often showed the various training methods that were used to forge the monk's skill. The program also offered Hollywood's conception of the psychological effects of this training.

The explosive growth of martial arts schools, the well-attended tournaments and the showing of martial arts movies and television programs all indicate a strong interest in Asian martial arts. Why are these arts coming into favor?

Martial Arts as Self-defense

ONE IMPORTANT reason for their popularity is the possible attainment of the ability to defend oneself against attack. Most of us have seen advertisements for schools of self-defense which say that a person trained in one of the Asian martial arts might be able, depending upon the system he has studied, to throw his attacker to the ground, render him helpless with some joint lock, or incapacitate him with a well-directed blow or kick. The allure of this kind of power for people who feel physically inadequate is evident when we reflect that in certain areas of many of our large cities those who walk the streets fear for their safety. Their fears are not unreasonable, because the crime rate in some neighborhoods is extremely high. However, most city areas are safe enough to permit us to go about our business in relative security. Nevertheless, if just one of our friends or acquaintances has been held up, mugged or even annoyed by hoodlums on the street, we begin to worry about our safety. The news media's instant and extensive coverage of untoward events feeds this fear. As a consequence of this climate of apprehension, those of us who are physically and mentally inclined toward defending ourselves might begin to prepare for possible violence at the hands of strangers. This preparation against attack might take the form of enrollment in a school of self-defense.

It is not always the danger of an overt physical attack that makes us uneasy about our safety. Almost everyone in our fast-paced, competitive society is faced daily with psychological pressures from others. Those with whom we associate often have interests in some measure opposed to ours and wish to have us embrace their views or further their interests. On the other hand, we may wish to convert others to our point of view. Although these encounters rarely extend beyond verbal expression, their impact on us is not without its physical side. Knowing that we could physically hold our own if the situation were to deteriorate in some way provides the confidence that is sometimes necessary if we are to avoid intimidation.

If we do enroll in a school of martial arts, what will we learn and how much time will we have to spend in order to attain an adequate degree of proficiency? Clearly, what is learned depends upon the kind of art we are studying. If we embark upon a judo program, our efforts will go toward learning to throw an opponent and render him helpless on the ground. Some throws, in which an opponent is raised almost shoulder high before he is brought down, look very spectacular. In other throws, the opponent's body describes only a small arc before hitting the mat. The criterion of effectiveness is that the opponent's back must hit the ground with sufficient force to incapacitate him if the surface were free of mats. From the self-defense standpoint, once the opponent is in the air he is helpless and can then be brought to the mat either on his back or on his head and shoulders.

The opponent does not merely stand still when under attack. He tries to evade and attempts attacks of his own. Theoretically, a throw is instigated because of some weakness in the opponent's position. If he attempts an attack which fails, his position often becomes vulnerable to a counterattack. However, the most commonly used method of weakening an opponent's position is by unbalancing him in some way. We can usually move in to perform our throw at the moment our opponent's balance is upset.

Some judo teachers teach a large number of throws and others confine themselves to only a few. A student must usually practice three times a week for about three years before he is considered to have secured a reasonable degree of skill in the performance of one throw. By "reasonable" is meant that he can usually throw an opponent with his technique even though the opponent, also a judo student, resists him. Of course, he should then have little trouble throwing an inexperienced assailant encountered in the street, provided that assailant is wearing clothing which resembles the jacket used in judo. Because he is accustomed to using the jacket for throwing, the student has difficulty in performing his technique against a person wearing only a light shirt.

Judo on the ground consists of holding the opponent so that he cannot escape. In addition, it is usually from this position that the opponent can be forced to give up if he is caught in a submission hold or a choke. Submission

16

holds are usually joint locks of the elbow or shoulder, with the threat of a dislocation of the joint if he fails to surrender. Chokes are strangulation techniques which, if correctly applied, cause unconsciousness within four or five seconds. Most chokes are done with the jacket collar, although methods of choking which make no use of the collar exist as well.

The foregoing content and approach to instruction is typical of most schools teaching sport judo. Some judo teachers also teach self-defense applications of sport techniques. They may also include the rudiments of kicking and punching. Nevertheless, the main emphasis is on throwing and grappling, especially where, as is usual, teachers expect their students to enter judo contests. Self-defense ability rises from this kind of training, despite the lack of emphasis on actual situations the student might meet in the street. To some extent this ability stems from an increase in physical strength and toughness. The body grows hard because it is accustomed to being thrown and to throwing others. The student becomes confident in his ability to throw someone if he can get his hands on him. He feels he can take a punch or two if necessary, get close enough to his opponent to secure a proper hold and, with his knowledge of throwing and grappling, quickly conclude the encounter.

Most people seeking a school of martial arts in order to learn to defend themselves would probably turn to one teaching some form of boxing. "Boxing" includes punching, striking and kicking, as well as blocking and parrying an opponent's offensive moves. In general, this method of fighting comes under the heading of karate or kung fu. Practitioners of these arts engage in a great deal of individual form practice as they strive to increase the speed and power of each technique. In training with a partner, punches and kicks usually are focused just short of the target. This practice prevents injury and yet does not greatly hamper the development of self-defense ability. Students of most karate and kung fu schools are also required to practice their punches, strikes and kicks against punching boards, heavy bags and wooden dummys in order to grow accustomed to the impact. In addition, by this means the striking surfaces of hands, feet, arms and legs are toughened. Some schools practice by having students wear protective padding, thereby avoiding the need for pulling punches and kicks. These various supplementary training devices ensure that the student will be able to deliver a strong attack if he decides to focus on the target instead of short of it.

Although two or three years of three times a week training at a karate school will give most people the means to easily defend themselves against the average unarmed assailant, real fighting ability is the result of another type of training. It requires, first of all, the kind of physical conditioning undertaken by serious amateur and professional boxers in the West. Running up to five miles almost every day is included in this training. Of primary importance, however, is hitting the opponent and being hit in return. Blocking and parrying and doing one's best to avoid an opponent's blows become of major importance if one wants to avoid injury. Sparring in karate seldom approaches this kind of intensity, although it is not unusual for punches to land on the target accidentally. In karate, the fact that he is occasionally hit maintains the kind of tension that helps keep the student's mind from wandering. Nevertheless, in most karate training, the ability to take punishment is not required to the same extent it is in some other forms of Eastern boxing.

In the "empty-hand" or weaponless fighting system spectrum, the soft or internal forms appear rather far removed from the hard karate or kung fu. Tai chi chuan, an example of an internal Chinese boxing system, seems at first glance of little use as self-defense. The first six to nine months of training are spent in learning a sequential series of movements, and it is only after this initial form has been learned that students begin to practice with one another. In daily practice, movements are usually done slowly. Breaking an opponent's balance or avoiding his push in the performance of push-hands does not seem much of an accomplishment to those who are accustomed to seeing people thrown to the ground or incapacitated by a well-aimed punch or kick.

Despite its ineffective appearance, a person adept at tai chi chuan is well able to cope with strong and fast attacks. Because he is relaxed, his movements can be made with startling quickness. The presence of tension in various parts of the body inhibits fast movement. Students of a hard boxing style like karate sometimes move relatively slowly because they are too tense. In addition, tai chi training bestows the ability to avoid an opponent's attack and at the same time deliver a counter. Unfortunately for those interested in quick results, tai chi chuan is technique-oriented and its teachers seek to avoid the use of strength to accomplish an end that should have been brought about by the use of sensitivity and timing. The growth and development of technique are slow. Thus, for those interested only in self-defense, two or three years spent in the study of tai chi chuan is just a beginning. It takes much longer to learn to cope successfully with a strong attack. Moreover, training must eventually include practice against fast and powerful attacks in order to accustom students to a realistic situation.

Aikido is related to tai chi chuan in that both systems emphasize the development and use of internal energy or power. However, aikido does not transmit this energy to a target by punching or kicking. Opponents are subdued primarily by twisting and locking their wrist, elbow or shoulder joints. The usual pattern of attack, defense and counterattack proceeds with an assailant attempting to hit, push or grasp the defender. The defender moves his body in such a way that the attacker overextends himself. Simultaneously, the defender grasps some convenient part of the attacker's body, usually his hand and wrist, and helps him in the direction his body is already moving. The attacker is not permitted to recover his balance, is thrown to the ground and forced to submit under threat of the dislocation of an arm or shoulder joint. Sometimes the attacker is thrown by the application of a body turn combined with the correct placement of a foot or leg, but usually the instant and intense pain of a joint lock makes him desperate to move in a direction that will lessen his agony. This direction is usually toward the ground.

It is important for beginners to be able to fall correctly, and once falling is learned, students begin to practice with one another. Classes proceed with a teacher's demonstration of a particular technique against some attack. Students then attempt to imitate the teacher's movements, partners taking attack and defense in turn. The best known form of aikido practices only prearranged techniques. However, some teachers of aikido have begun allowing students to engage in free play, in which a defender's counter might in turn be countered by the attacker until one or the other is forced to submit.

Aikido techniques are usually performed in response to an assailant's offensive move. Thus, they are defensive in nature, and aikido often appeals to beginners who might be repelled by the more aggressive appearance of some of the other martial arts. Of course, the aikido student could always goad another person into attacking him so that the attacker could fall victim to an aikido technique. But this procedure need not be followed if the aikidoist determined his best course of action lay in attacking first. In this case, it would be easy enough for him to reach out to grasp an opponent's arm or hand and then apply some technique. Thus, although aikido is usually practiced as a defensive movement against an actual attack, it can also be used to forestall what might be considered an impending attack. At any rate, it receives high marks in terms of its usefulness as defense against an unarmed assailant.

Judo, karate, Chinese boxing of various kinds and aikido are the various forms of Eastern martial arts generally taught and most easily found in our large cities. All of them are basically unarmed fighting systems, although to some degree they may include training in various weapons. Weapons training in those systems that teach it runs from the use of sharp-edged metal throwing devices to swords, but excludes firearms.

Martial arts schools that teach weapons exclusively are rare in the United States. However, a Japanese martial art based on sword fighting, but practiced as a sport, is slowly gaining followers. This sport is kendo. Kendoists wear protective equipment to prevent injury and wield a "sword" fashioned of split bamboo called a *shinai*. The Japanese sword is a two-handed weapon and the *shinai* is usually held with two hands. Targets are limited to an opponent's wrist, chest, head and throat. Attacks must be correctly focused to score. Students are taught to evade an opponent's attack by moving their body and by blocking and parrying. Because the end of the *shinai* moves extremely fast, a kendoist's reflexes become exceedingly sharp. His reaction to the fleeting appearance of some opening in an opponent's defense or his response to attack must be instantaneous if he is to be reasonably successful. Thus, after a few years training, a kendoist equipped with a stout stick would experience little difficulty in dealing with an unarmed assailant or even an attacker wielding a knife.

Some kendo schools may also teach iaido, a method of drawing a sword from its scabbard and cutting or thrusting with it. This draw is an attacking maneuver and is performed against an imaginary opponent. Emphasis is placed on performing all actions with full concentration, a stipulation underscored by the fact that the practitioner is using a live sword which can easily inflict injury if it is clumsily handled.

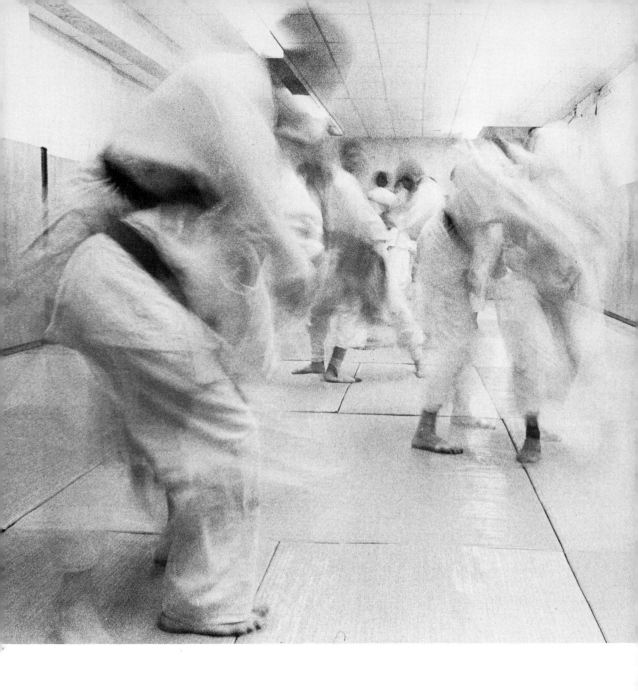

Martial Arts as Physical Exercise

ANOTHER major reason for the growing attractiveness of martial arts is the physical exercise each student must perform. As we practice various techniques with or without a partner, we place demands on our body that go far beyond those usually experienced in everyday living. This additional physical exertion is especially marked in those with sedentary jobs whose leisure-time activities before they began studying a martial art consisted of watching television or reading.

Beyond the fact that we seem to feel better when we exercise on a regular basis, individuals who have studied the effect of exercise on the body are almost unanimous in saying that without exercise our health will begin to deteriorate. Put in a positive way, writers on physical fitness maintain that those who exercise regularly (at least three times a week for one hour per period) have better blood circulation, better muscle tone and fewer illnesses than those who abstain from such activity. Because of the high incidence of diseases of the heart and circulatory systems in developed countries, most authorities on fitness have concerned themselves with the effect of exercise on the circulatory system. They generally share the opinion that if we are to avoid heart disease, the heart must be given work beyond the minimal demands made on it by sedentary living.

It is not only the lack of physical activity that contributes to the onset of ill health. The stressful psychological conditions under which many of us carry on our lives are usually also detrimental to good health. Mental and emotional tension, if it is too great or too prolonged, often manifests itself in some physical ailment. Researchers on the effect of stress on people's health have found that this phenomenon is one of the chief causes of heart disease and other major illnesses. The findings are that those who share certain personality traits—the hard-driving, highly competitive persons—are more susceptible to harmful stress than individuals who take an easygoing attitude toward life. If we are stress-prone, what can we do to redue stress or counter its injurious effects? Although they fail to agree unanimously, scientists

23

seeking ways to reduce the harmful effect of stress on people have recommended exercise.

Some of us need an outlet for our frustrations and our hostile impulses. In our everyday lives we must deal with problems that often defy quick or easy solution. Usually our round of daily activities begins with commuting to work by automobile or public transport. In our larger cities, rush hour traffic is usually congested and public transport is crowded. Bumper to bumper traffic, moving slowly or not at all is not conducive to a relaxed state of mind. Subways and buses during the rush hour are usually uncomfortably packed as they move us, with periodic delays, towards our destination. These conditions are upsetting and aggravating. The jobs we go to often fail to satisfy us in important ways, but we must stick to them in order to earn enough to support ourselves and our family. The journey home is rarely more pleasant than the trip to work. Often problems connected with house and family must be faced after the working day. Of course, most people's lives have their bright side and the unpleasant aspects must be viewed in proper perspective. Nevertheless, the aggravating and frustrating experiences that we must suffer as a result of living in our urban environment leaves a residue of anger and hostility which must have an outlet if we are to maintain our health. Physical exercise is an excellent way to relieve these harmful feelings.

We might also view the problem of frustration and its accompanying anger and hostility from the standpoint of society's health. These feelings may be turned inward upon ourselves or we may direct them outward upon those around us. Often both processes seem to be operating in those of us afflicted in this way. If we favor the first method we usually live in a kind of crippled way. Our mind and probably our body are usually to some degree impaired. Naturally, society is weakened when individuals, who constitute the threads in this fabric, break down in some way. If we choose the second method and act unkindly or offensively toward others, the result is often traumatic for them and further serves to impede a smoothly functioning society. Keeping society healthy, in a manner of speaking, through the avoidance of unnecessary mental or physical breakdown in its members or friction between them is a by-product of physical exercise.

The training done in martial arts provides this physical exercise. But the energy generated by this anger and hostility is not merely released through this training. Instead, the energy is used to further the student's self-development and self-realization. Such training cannot help but benefit those who engage in it. Ultimately the society these individuals form is also strengthened.

As we practice martial arts, we find that our training has a strong effect upon our mind as well as on our body. Over the months and years, we usually grow increasingly conscious of ourselves as a unit, all parts of which must work together harmoniously if we are to remain healthy. Therefore we might begin to think of our health in a way that differs from the customary Western pattern. We usually depend upon a member of the medical profession to cure us after an illness has been allowed to progress to a point that calls for intensive measures. Instead of waiting for our health to deteriorate to this level before doing something, we might give more attention to the prevention of illness. For example, as we become aware of the functioning of our body, we may notice a negative reaction toward certain foods. Our diet may change until our body signals us, by an increase of energy or the feeling of general well-being, that we are eating correctly.

Acceptance of the concept of body-mind unity makes us more concerned than previously with ways the body affects the mind and vice-versa. Thus we could become aware, if the condition existed, of the bad effect on our health of certain of our relationships with others. Perhaps our working environment is contributing to a health problem. Usually we find ourselves unable to withdraw from these situations, but knowing of their potential danger to our health, we might seek ways to reduce the incidence and severity of stressful encounters. Sometimes a change in our attitude about ourselves or others helps reduce this harmful tension. Our martial arts training helps alleviate this kind of stress, but a wiser approach would be to take steps to prevent its appearance.

For those who have let the years go by without using their body in ways that cause muscles to strain, the heart to pump rapidly and the lungs to demand greater amounts of air, a class in martial arts may seem too demanding. They know they need more exercise because their body sends them daily signals in the form of vague discomfort and general malaise. Yet the strenuous activity characteristic of most martial arts classes seems beyond their capabilities. A good teacher will, however, take the beginner along slowly, placing demands on him which he can meet. The beginner's capacity for exertion will grow gradually until he is able to keep pace with the rest of the class. Of course, this procedure is not without its aches and pains. There might even be times when the beginner will feel his teacher is asking him to do more than he can, but to his surprise he will find himself able to do it. In the course of six months the new student will find accumulated fat disappearing from his midsection. The muscles of his body will regain their firmness. He will be able to sustain a high rate of physical activity for some minutes without excessive pulse rate or breathlessness. He will get pleasure from regaining the use of his body and from knowing that he can rely upon it in some emergency. Finally, the link between body and mind will be more strongly established and its existence underscored. Only as the body receives its full share of attention can we begin to approach that harmonious interplay of body and mind expressed as an important ideal by outstanding thinkers of the past. If we neglect our body in the belief that its importance ranks considerably below our mental activity, it will usually have its revenge in the form of the appearance of some manner of illness.

If we have been ill or for some other reason find ourselves unable to enter upon a strenuous physical training program, such martial arts as tai chi chuan or aikido pursue a gentler and more gradual path. In tai chi, the leg muscles must do a considerable amount of work because individual form and push-hands with a partner are done with knees bent in a kind of quarter squat. However, the emphasis on daily practice and strictures against forcing anything result in a more gradual development of the student's strength and ability than is usual in the more strenuous martial arts like judo and the various forms of boxing.

Many of us who recognize the benefits of exercise and realize that we are in poor physical shape might embark on some course of exercise for a certain period to try to regain a pleasing physical appearance or to lose weight. Once we have effected some cosmetic change we might return to our old habits, hoping that we will not deteriorate too quickly. However, exercise cannot be stored. To maintain optimum health, our body should receive some form of exercise each day. Working out for a few months each year is not as beneficial as maintaining an exercise program throughout the year. Exercising only on weekends often does more harm than good, because it places an unaccustomed strain on the body.

Learning one of the martial arts is an excellent way to get the exercise our body requires. If the exercise we do is boring, we find it increasingly difficult to spend the required time plugging away at it. Calesthenics fall into this category. Running laps around a track or swimming from one end of a pool to another may become mentally tiresome. Jogging over changing terrain is interesting for some, but weather conditions sometimes prohibit this form of exercise. Few activities are as interesting as some form of martial arts training. If a beginner has based his decision to learn a martial art only on his desire for a good workout, he soon finds that he is training because the art itself has caught his interest. He may notice that it is engaging his mind as well as his body and providing unexpected insight into himself and others.

Martial Arts as Meditation

STILL ANOTHER aspect of martial arts considered of major consequence is meditation. It has been said that, properly taught, both individual form practice and training with a partner constitute moving meditation. Beginners interested in this facet of martial arts may have read of the experiences of men who have trained in some form of martial art with a Zen master, and they may want to undergo the development written about. Others attracted by meditation may think sitting in a static posture somewhat dull in comparison with executing the crisp actions of a karate *kata* (form) or performing the flowing, slowly unfolding sequential movements of the tai chi form.

Those who begin martial arts training in the hope of reaping some of the benefits that come from meditation must, of course, find a teacher who favors and understands this aspect of training. Unfortunately, a beginner's notion of what this kind of training encompasses is usually wide of the mark. He may feel that his reading or his ideas on this subject have prepared him sufficiently to make a valid judgment concerning a teacher's methods. If the teacher proceeds in a way that fails to square with the beginner's preconceptions, some disappointment or perhaps even disillusionment may occur. The student may feel that he is not being taught as he should be, although his conception of the whole matter is intellectual and theoretical and lacks the grounding of experience. It is only as he continues to practice over the months and years and sees himself changing in ways he may not have anticipated that he begins to gain respect for his teacher's methods.

Unfortunately, another danger presents itself as students start to feel this respect. They may begin to rely too much on the teacher and expect him to do the work only they can do. It is, of course, fitting that a teacher receive respect, appreciation and loyalty from his students. He has something valuable to offer in his knowledge and experience. He is willing to share this and can point the way for those willing to listen to him. But students should not expect too much of him. He is human and should not be deified. Nor should students think that being in his presence or listening to his advice will solve their problems for them. Each of us must be self-reliant. We should not become overly dependent on another person for the attainment of outer or inner growth. If we do establish such dependency, we will find, sooner or later, that we have taken a wrong turning.

Most students come to the martial arts for self-defense training or for exercise. If they begin to encounter a different emphasis in their training, they may not understand what is intended. The self-defense will be there, physical training will be done in full measure, and aggressive drives and frustrations will find an outlet. But as their training progresses, they may find that their teacher considers of primary importance such intangibles as self-knowledge and, ultimately, self-realization.

Western students of Asian martial arts usually are unaware that the Eastern view of man differs from their own. In general, Asian thought about man does not divide him into body and mind, as has been true for hundreds and perhaps thousands of years in the West. In the East, body and mind combine to form the individual. Thus, man is considered as a unit. Martial arts teachers who share this view see themselves as helping their students develop as a whole. In teaching what Westerners would consider physical skills, they think they are affecting the student's mental and psychological approach to life as well as cultivating his body. Therefore when a Western student begins to notice that his teacher seems to be concerned with more than his physical development, he should not be surprised. It is not so much that this kind of teacher deals with the student's mind, an area which Westerners might think the affair of the psychiatrist or someone of that sort, but that the teacher considers the student in his totality.

Students in the West sometimes disagree with this approach to their training. Perhaps they feel the study of martial arts should be concerned only with its practical application. Those who train in a martial art that stresses competition may think winning is of first importance. Such thinking seems to view martial arts too narrrowly and is usually held by beginners and by students whose teachers themselves think in this way. However, those who have practiced some years and are still unaware of anything beyond the physical miss the vast potential in their training that can contribute to self-knowledge. Becoming more aware of how we think and feel about ourselves is the first and perhaps most important step in changing our lives for the better.

In Western terms, martial arts training can then be considered as concerned with inner development as well as outer. The various kinds of individual form practice done in all martial arts are not only skill-producing but meditative in that they still the logical, rational portion of the brain and allow us to relate to life with other areas of our mind. Moreover, important information which may be buried in what is usually termed the subconscious is, through this kind of practice, permitted to surface. Our training is not, however, designed merely to bring this hidden information to our consciousness. It also helps us to begin to face and deal with our problems by learning control and discipline. Once we know ourselves we can begin to control tendencies which have proved of negative value in the past and to emphasize aspects of our makeup that seem to take us in the direction we feel we want our lives to go. Achieving these results is, however, the product of years of steady training.

30

CHAPTER II

What Kind of Martial Art Should be Studied?

ASIAN MARTIAL ARTS include a wide range of systems. At one extreme are those in which students perform stylized, dance-like movements that seem to bear little resemblance in form or spirit to a fighting art. The rationale behind such practice seems to be that modern man does not have to prepare himself to fight in the same way he did in past centuries. However, he does need physical training to maintain his health. In addition, the performance of the intricate gymnastics involved in this kind of practice pleases his aesthetic sense. At the other extreme are weapons sytems in which the emphasis is on preparing for combat. These systems require of their students intensive daily training in all weathers and on all kinds of terrain.

How does the beginner decide which of these arts he wants to study? The following discussion proceeds on the assumption that the beginner has a reasonably large selection of systems available to him. (Many of our large cities presently offer a fairly wide range of systems.) Moreover, let us assume that teachers of each particular art are teaching in the same way and are of equal merit, although this is never the case. In actual practice, the beginner would do his best to eliminate from consideration those systems in which the teachers in question fail to teach in a way he thinks will help him realize his objectives. Unfortunately, beginners sometimes are unclear about their objectives or about their reasons for wanting to study martial arts. Often they begin their practice expecting one kind of training only to be surprised, sometimes pleasantly, that the surface appearance of the training is a kind of illusion and that something unexpected and valuable is happening to them. Sometimes this "hidden" kind of training is what they were actually seeking, but they were not consciously aware of the fact.

Class Procedure

THOSE WHO have never studied a martial art might be curious about class procedure and structure. A brief, general description of the atmosphere that prevails at various schools may help to satisfy this curiosity. Clearly, the range in terms of formality and intensity of training is quite broad. Formality at some schools may be severe, with classes taught as they would be in the East, including ceremonial bows toward a shrine and toward the teacher at the start and finish of each practice session. While students and teacher are sitting in formal positions on the floor, a brief period of meditation might precede the final bows. Students also bow to one another at the beginning and end of each sparring session, perhaps using the polite phrase that translates "Would you do me the honor of practicing with me?" when they start and expressing thanks as they finish.

In this kind of class, a hierarchy exists with the teacher at the top and students ranked by grade and length of experience. Beginners are taken in hand by senior students and told, sometimes harshly, what is expected of them. A transgression against the prescribed way of doing things, such as showing disrespect toward the teacher or toward a senior student, is dealt with by senior students or the teacher by intensifying the training for the offender. Rules and regulations are not usually spelled out and it is up to the beginner to be careful. An unusually heavy practice session with a senior student in which the beginner is worked almost to exhaustion or is taken to task about his less than adequate efforts should cause him to reflect on his behavior and to change quickly what might be offensive. If he is unable or unwilling to change his behavior, he drops out or is asked to leave by the teacher.

In sharp contrast are those schools or clubs where formality is at a minimum. Bowing is nonexistent and teacher-student and senior student-beginner relationships are conducted on a level of near equality. Of course, teachers and senior students are considered to have more knowledge and ability than beginners in the art they are practicing. They are respected for this, but respect or deference does not extend beyond the area in which they possess expertise. Usually in schools of this kind there is little if any feeling on the part of anyone that something more is being imparted than the intricacies of technique leading to the attainment of skill. This situation might exist among students interested only in competing in judo or karate contests. These students are mainly concerned with perfecting their skill and need training partners with whom to practice and a teacher who can give them additional ideas on technique.

The intensity of practice also varies from school to school. All Asian martial arts include a large percentage of drill in the various techniques that must be learned. To become proficient in his art, a student must repeat movements thousands of times with and without a partner. If judo is studied, the movements of a particular throw are repeated endlessly over the months and years until the action necessary is automatic and reflexive. In karate, the various kicks, punches and blocks that comprise the art must be internalized and are therefore practiced daily over the years. This pattern of seemingly endless repetition is found in all schools of martial arts. But one group may be interested only in getting a reasonable amount of exercise a few times each week. It is obvious that the members of this school would not be working too hard. Another may want to have its members win trophies in contests and attempts to insure victory by training harder than other groups with similar aims. Still another might be intent on some kind of inner development and fashions its training to achieve that end. Those interested in beginning some form of martial arts training should determine the seriousness of purpose that prevails in the schools they visit, as well as the intensity with which it is pursued, and choose a group that accords with their interests.

Weapons Systems

A USEFUL DIVISION among the martial arts separates systems that train only with weapons from those that concentrate on dealing with an armed or unarmed opponent with weaponless techniques. Some empty-hand systems include training with weapons after a student has achieved some degree of skill in the basic method of attacking and defending. Although a weapon is used, it is considered an extension of the hand, and movements are made in the manner characteristic of the weaponless system. Thus, despite some practice with weapons, the emphasis continues to be on learning empty-hand techniques. These systems would not, therefore, belong in the "weapons" category.

What advantages lie in studying a weapons system instead of a system that teaches only empty-hand techniques? Let us assume for the moment that this question deals only with the possibility of developing some kind of useful skill as contrasted with training that might extend beyond this. Studying a weapons system might appeal to a person who is concerned with his safety or with defending himself from attack. Some people live in or must visit parts of the city where the crime rate is high. Faced with this situation, they may feel safer if they have been trained in the use of a weapon.

Others attracted to the study of a weapons system might feel that practicing with a weapon instills a more serious attitude toward training than is found in weaponless systems. Theoretically, weapons systems continue to teach the utilitarian and practical methods of dispatching an enemy in hand-to-hand fighting. Movements are not stylized or changed in a way that might enhance the appearance of the form which they comprise. Practice is not confined to an indoor hall but is conducted as much as possible in all kinds of weather and on a surface that might be encountered in combat.

Unfortunately, few opportunities exist for people in the United States who want to study a weapons system. In the rare instances where they do, the weapons studied are the sword and the stick. Although training in either of these weapons would enable a student to more than hold his own in combat against one or more unarmed assailants or one armed with a knife or a club, a sword or stick would be inadequate against an attacker armed with a pistol. It is true that a man trained in the use of sword or stick is not without resource against one armed with a pistol, especially if the latter is unskilled in the use of the pistol and if the confrontation is at close quarters. Nevertheless, in general, the advantage would clearly seem to be with the man armed with a pistol.

Another problem confronting those who might be apprehensive enough about their safety to want to study a weapons system concerns the legality of the use of a weapon to resist attack. It is clearly illegal to carry a sword about. However, a stick or cane might legally be carried as an aid in walking. But even though we have the right to defend ourselves from attack, the question of using more force than necessary in fighting off an assailant could enter the picture. Of course, we would probably be justified in using whatever means we had at our disposal to defend against unprovoked attack, especially if the motive were robbery and the attacker possessed a weapon. But situations differ, and whenever we employ a weapon in self-defense and our assailant sustains serious injury the charge might be made that we overstepped the bounds of a sufficient and reasonable degree of force.

The conclusion that appears to follow from the foregoing argument is that those attracted to the study of a weapons system because of a preoccupation with self-defense might reflect further concerning the practicality of such a choice.

Sport vs. Non-sport Systems

For MOST prospective students, a more obvious and available choice in martial arts is between a sportive system and one in which they need not participate in contests. Judo is an example of the former, while aikido or tai chi chuan might represent the latter.

Judo got its start in Japan in the 1880's through the efforts of Jigoro Kano. He had spent years studying various jujitsu styles and decided to construct a system of his own, the movements of which could be practiced by young and old of both sexes. Originally it was designed as a means of strengthening the population of Japan both physically and mentally. In its early formulation, judo included the sparing use of contests as part of an overall training of mind and body. Kano recognized the value of allowing students to periodically test their progress under the stress of a contest situation. As the years went by and judo spread from Japan to other parts of the world, the idea gradually took hold that a student's ability in judo could be gauged by his success in contests. Viewed another way, judo became a sport and the idea of working toward mental and physical perfection gradually became of secondary importance, when it was not altogether forgotten.

As a consequence of this trend, most present-day judo teachers prepare their students for participation in contests. Whatever the particular idea they may have concerning their students' inner development, if they are members of a regional judo organization, it is usually expected that their students participate in the contests that these organizations schedule throughout the year. Students' promotions also depend in large part on their success in contests, and the regional organization will plan a number of special promotional contests through the year. If a judo teacher opposes this way of doing things and does not allow his students to take part in contests, he will be thought by other judo instructors and players to be teaching an inferior brand of judo, if in fact they term it judo at all. Moreover, his students' ranking would not be recognized outside of his training hall.

Judo is organized on a regional, national and international basis. Although disagreements of one sort or another sometimes arise between factions in the various organizations, success in contests of individuals and teams seems the standard by which the prestige of a club, region or nation is measured. Most judo instructors teaching today were raised in this system, and many of the older ones were instrumental in helping it take its present form. These teachers and their students therefore conduct their training in a way that will help them win contests.

In this country twenty-five years ago, it was the rare student who practiced each day for an hour or two. A one-to-two-hour training period was usually held only three days a week. However, in those days the number of judo players in the country and in the world was much smaller than at

present. At that time, Japanese players were thought to be more dedicated and reports were that they trained daily and workouts were strenuous. Currently, with the strong emphasis on competition, serious students in this country practice almost daily. Moreover, they run a few miles each morning to build stamina and many lift weights to increase strength. Nor do they neglect technique. Their objective is to develop into the kind of player who combines good technique with speed, strength and endurance. An additional factor in such a player's development is seasoning — knowing one's way about the mat. This kind of knowledge is gained in tournaments, and teachers usually have their students enter as many contests as possible in order to broaden their experience.

In contrast to the highly organized, contest-oriented sport system that judo has become, some martial arts are restricted to training only within the school. Among these are to be found weapons systems that do not lend themselves to a sporting application because of the almost certain danger of serious injury to the participants. Other examples of systems that avoid contests are the Uyeshiba system of aikido and some forms of tai chi chuan. Often these non-sport systems express strong concern for a student's mental and moral, as well as for his physical, development.

It should be clear that the pattern of training in a martial arts system in which students avoid participation in contests will differ from one that encourages or requires such participation. In general, the noncompetitive systems might be described as devoting considerable attention to perfecting technique. Technique receives its share of emphasis in a sport system, but if the result sought can be achieved by the use of additional strength or by moving more quickly than the opponent, most practitioners are satisfied. This is not usually true of the non-sport systems. Practice is concerned with achieving a particular objective — pushing an opponent off-balance, applying a joint lock, evading an attack — with a very minimum of physical strength. On the other hand, the contest-oriented group, in general, is interested in immediate results. Thus, in a tournament situation, if the application of additional strength or speed to a technique will overcome an opponent's resistance, every effort will be made to exert that extra physical effort.

Sometimes techniques that comprise a particular form become stylized to an extent that negates their practical value in fighting. In other words, a sequential form might at the outset have been based upon combative techniques, but over the years it receives a new stress concerned with smoothness of execution or continuity. Of course, this need not occur, but the possibility exists where practitioners do not periodically encounter tests of the efficacy of their technique.

Internal vs. External Styles

THE TERMS "internal" and "external" to describe fighting systems generally have been used to refer to divisions between the boxing styles of China. An excellent discussion of the differences between these styles as well as their historical development appears in Drager and Smith's *Asian Fighting Arts*. This distinction is also valuable and useful when applied to the martial arts of other countries. Thus, many Japanese and Korean karate styles would be considered external or "hard," while the Chinese tai chi chuan or Japanese aikido would be termed internal or "soft."

The rationale behind the training encountered in the external style is that the body must be able to bring maximum physical power to bear on a target in attacking and defending. This power is not thought to be produced in any mysterious way. Hard style boxing practitioners use the leg muscles to thrust their feet into the ground as strongly as possible and allow the power generated by this thrust to flow into the lower abdominal area and hips. Then they rotate the body in a way that will permit the force generated by the legs to flow through the rest of the body into the arm and onto the target. The muscles used in the movement are brought into play as necessary and are tensed or focused at the moment of impact. Because quickness of delivery is an important factor in achieving power, techniques are usually performed with maximum speed. In attacking, the object often is to drive through any obstruction on the way to the target. The student is expected to toughen himself enough, by repeatedly striking an opponent's arm as he attacks and defends, to eventually suffer no feeling of pain despite very hard contact with some bony part of an opponent's body.

Those who practice a hard style often do supplementary physical exercise to strengthen the body's muscles. Squatting and springing into the air, hopping about while squatting and holding a low stance for a long period of time, sometimes while supporting another student on one's shoulders, are some of the exercises used to increase leg power. Push-ups, perhaps with added weight on the shoulders, strengthen the arms. Sit-ups build the muscles of the abdominal region. Occasionally weights are liften to strengthen shoulders and back. Moreover, the body is hardened as well as strengthened. The knuckles and other parts of the hand used in punching or striking are toughened and hardened by hitting padded boards or sandbags. The forearms, used in blocking, and the shins are also toughened, if not by striking a padded surface, then by contact with an attacker's arm or leg while sparring. To build stamina, some students run a few miles each day or engage in protracted periods of form practice or training with a partner. Flexibility is not neglected and each training session sees its portion of bending and stretching.

When sparring with an opponent, exponents of an external style try to stay relaxed and to move about as required in defense or attack. In punching or blocking, students try to focus their strength on the target in the split second in which the opportunity affords itself and then release this focus in preparation for the following technique. For example, if his first punch or kick is strongly blocked by the defensive movement of his opponent, the attacker must instantly switch to his next technique if he wants to successfully complete his attack. His assessment of the situation—that the defender's block is too strong for his attack to succeed—must come at the very moment the block is executed. In the next split second the attacker must perform a followup to prevent the defender from countering. Movements are powerfully executed in an attempt to break the opponent's balance so that he is unable either to defend or to launch a successful followup technique. Although opponents try to avoid an attack by removing themselves from its path, such evasive action is usually combined with a block or parry.

The internal or "soft" boxing style, of which tai chi chuan is a foremost example, avoids attempting to build the kind of muscular strength described above. The legs are expected to become powerful, however, because in theory their function is to provide a strong foundation and support for the rest of the body in whatever physical endeavor a person engages. The sequential form that must be practiced daily is done throughout with bent knees, forcing the leg muscles to work. As for the rest of the body, movements are usually performed slowly and rhythmically with only the minimum strength employed to fulfill the requirements of the position. The emphasis is on relaxation. In addition, this relaxed body helps to promote the flow of internal energy called *chi* in Chinese or *ki* in Japanese. A reservoir of this energy is said to lie in the lower abdominal area and, once developed and controlled, *chi* or *ki* can be used in attack and defense.

Practitioners of the internal style claim that the use of this internal energy is more effective in prevailing over an opponent than is the use of the kind of strength advocated by exponents of external systems. Teachers and students of external systems obviously find it difficult to accept this claim. Their training has made them physically strong. This power coupled with their mastery of technique enables them to perform seemingly impossible feats in throwing, grappling, kicking and punching. They are willing to accept the role of the mind in what they do in the sense of achieving full concentration. But they are unwilling to credit more than body dynamics and the correct application of the principles of leverage with their results. Tests of the superiority of one method over the other seem to be inconclusive. One can see the results of the application of a technique, but beyond the outward appearance of body movement the method by which a martial artist of either system achieves his objective is difficult to determine. A verbal account by the performer often lacks clarity and sometimes borders on the mystical.

Training with a partner in the internal style generally proceeds using the relaxed body, minimal strength and low center of gravity learned in individual form practice. Called push-hands, this training method calls for the attacker to push the defender off balance while the defender seeks to evade the attack and simultaneously unbalance the attacker. It is usually performed from a fixed stance. Any change of foot position on the part of the defender is presumed caused by an inability to evade the attack and signifies a loss of balance. In order to develop their ability to handle an attack while they are in motion, more advanced students sometimes forego a fixed stance and practice push-hands while advancing and retreating.

Throughout this practice, partners usually move slowly. The defender attempts to develop his ability to sense the direction and force of an attack,

while his opponent tries to follow as closely as possible the evasive movements attempted by the defense. Compared with the external style method of evading an attack, the internal style relies much more on pliability and yielding. Hard or strong blocking movements are almost never used. As concerns timing, the adversaries both seek the correct moment for the delivery of an attack or the initiation of an evasive maneuver. Timing is also important in learning to focus a surge of energy onto the target. One aspect of training, whether alone or with a partner, is directed toward furthering the ability to release this kind of energy at the right moment.

Comparison of National Styles or Systems

IT IS REASONABLE to expect the empty-hand fighting systems of one country to differ in various ways from those of another. Those fighting systems native to a country differ from those of another country because in past centuries the exchange of ideas and techniques proceeded relatively slowly. Consequently, a native system would have had a chance to develop in its own way. This development would be strongly influenced by the attitude toward life held by the people of the country in question. Thus, an empty-hand fighting system of Japan would differ from a Chinese one in ways that would reflect the general culture dominant in each country. In addition, elements of or complete fighting systems brought in from other countries would, over time, be similarly influenced.

This point might be kept in mind by Westerners as they decide which system of martial arts to study. The cultural characteristics of a country will be most evident in a system native to that country or, if the system has been imported, only when it has been taught in its new environment for several generations. Moreover, if taught in the West, a system of this kind is mostly likely to retain its particular cultural flavor for at least a generation if the teacher is a native of the foreign land or a Westerner who has studied the art in its native environment or in some other way absorbed the essentials of the foreign culture. In the latter case, the degree to which it is possible for a Westerner to reflect the intricacies of an Eastern culture is questionable, if it is even considered desirable. Yet in those important areas of human life that are universal, Eastern methods of arriving at understanding are clearly within the capacity of Westerners to absorb and to pass on. At any rate, Westerners who might be interested in or attracted to the culture of China might select a Chinese martial art. Those who are drawn to a Japanese view of things would find the martial arts system of that country reflecting this view.

Who Can Study?

THE DESCRIPTIONS of the strenuous and perhaps violent activity that takes place in some of the martial arts may cause some readers to conclude that the study of those particular systems is not for them. This conclusion is probably warranted in the case of persons whose physiques are unusually frail or who suffer from some physical ailment that would be aggravated by rough body contact. However, a person who is reasonably healthy and whose body works as it should need not feel apprehensive about embarking on a study of any martial art. This statement is made with the provision that the teacher of the art is a good one, interested in his students' welfare. In addition, a serious study of the more strenuous arts should not, in general, be initiated before the ages of thirteen or fourteen and after the ages of forty or forty-five. From the physical standpoint, the sometimes extreme stress on some of the body's joints might be harmful to a person who has not fully matured. At the other end of the scale, an older person's body begins to lose its resiliency and may be harmed by such hard usage.

In the foregoing paragraph, no distinction was made concerning the sex of prospective students. At the present time in this country, most martial arts schools accept women as students. They usually undergo the same training as men. However, they are not permitted to compete with men in contests in those arts that are sport-oriented. Despite this restriction, the important point is that women are not automatically barred from participation in martial arts training on the basis of their sex. The physical and mental demands of the various martial arts are in a sense the final criteria as to who

is attracted and who remains. Those who are drawn to this training and find it rewarding and beneficial will continue to practice. Those who begin but feel unable to continue, for whatever reason, will drop out.

We have been discussing participation in relation to the more strenuous martial arts, such as judo and karate. But persons interested in studying a martial art need not confine themselves to those. They can ultimately derive the same benefits from a study of the softer and gentler arts, such as aikido or tai chi chuan. Even persons well along in years (sixties or seventies) or those who are physically below par can derive valuable physical and mental benefits from a study of the rhythmic and gentle form practice done in tai chi chuan.

Without, hopefully, overstating the case, almost everyone can benefit from a study of one of the martial arts. However, prospective students must carefully consider what they are able and willing to endure and then choose wisely.

CHAPTER III

The Aim of Individual Form Practice

Developing Skill

IN MOST of the martial arts, students are taught to move in ways that sometimes appear difficult and even unnatural at first. As they observe the movements of a skilled practitioner, they are impressed with the grace, power and flow of each technique. Their own efforts seem awkward by comparison. Learning to move in the manner suggested by their teacher may call for placing the feet and legs in positions that feel uncomfortable, using the hands in unaccustomed or unusual ways and maintaining a perpendicular body despite its desire to incline in various directions. These initial difficulties are often caused by the beginner's lack of previous physical training. His body may be tense, with stiff muscles and shortened tendons and ligaments. These need to be stretched if he is to achieve the necessary range in his movements. Sometimes his arms or legs are too weak to allow him to pull or push as much as is necessary. He may have trouble bending his knees to the correct degree and for the amount of time required. This lack of basic physical ability hampers the beginner in his attempt to learn to use his body in the prescribed way. Nevertheless, as he persists in his efforts he will gradually overcome his deficiencies and his body will begin to respond to his direction as

49

it should.

In most systems, students practice the various techniques they would use against an opponent without the participation of a partner. The degree to which such solo practice is done varies from art to art. Those martial arts that require a partner for practicing such movements as throwing, grappling or joint locks make only limited use of individual practice. In judo, for example, a beginner will first learn to fall in various directions. He does this from sitting, squatting and standing positions, without a partner. As he improves, he may jump into the air, turn a somersault and land on his back without ill effect, breaking his fall in the recommended manner. After he has learned to fall from a respectable height without injury, his teacher or a more experienced student will begin to throw him into the air to allow him to become accustomed to falling when someone is throwing him.

When he can fall correctly, he is taught the mechanics of one or more throwing techniques. In this procedure, the beginner usually performs the technique he is learning with only the imaginary presence of a partner. The footwork combined with the pull and the turn of the body can profitably be done thousands of times without a partner until the movement becomes almost a reflex that occurs in the split second in which an opening occurs. At first, of course, the technique is performed slowly with emphasis on the correct positioning of all parts of the body. This kind of individual practice is useful for the duration of a person's judo training. To simulate an opponent's resistance, the student might also tie his judo uniform belt around a tree or post and pull on the belt as he practices his throw.

Individual training of this nature enables the student to grow accustomed to the body mechanics involved in the performance of his techniques. He is not distracted by an opponent's shifting about evasively or attempting to counterattack. He has time in which to work on problems concerned with correct foot placement, body position or pulling direction. In an actual match, the opportunity to perform a throw appears only briefly, allowing insufficient time to give attention to the many factors involved. Certain optimum patterns of movement must be established, and these can only become set if they are repeated almost endlessly. Nevertheless, because judo techniques are performed while maintaining contact with an opponent, as students progress they tend to forego individual practice for practice with a partner. In a sense, however, this practice can still be considered individual because the partner may be asked to cooperate, thereby enabling the student to strengthen and polish his movements.

Because karate training does not involve as much physical contact with an opponent—throwing and grappling are minimal in most styles—it makes more use of individual form practice than judo does. Countless hours are spent in moving forward and backward over the floor while delivering punches, blocks and kicks. At the outset, the fundamentals of each technique are carefully taught. Foot position of the stance, knee placement and hip and body rotation in a punching or striking technique are all described in detail. The route of the foot in the delivery of the various kicks and that of the hand in strikes, punches and blocks is demonstrated until the student knows what is required. Once these rudiments of positioning and movement have been learned, it is up to each student to correctly perform each technique with maximum speed and power. Every training session has a period of time devoted to drilling in the basic techniques used in karate. It is thought that success in more advanced karate training, such as the delivery of techniques in combination or the almost simultaneous application of block and counter characteristic of freestyle sparring, depends upon the correct performance of basic movements.

Kata Practice

THESE BASIC movements are also combined in a sequential form called *kata* in Japanese. Students must memorize a number of these sequences over the months and years of their training. In such *kata,* the performer blocks and counters various attacks delivered by a number of imaginary assailants located at different spots around him. Often the *kata* as a whole has a certain overriding theme or idea which the student attempts to express as he does the required moves. At the periodic promotional contests, an examining board of teachers grades each student on his performance of one or more of these forms. As his skill increases, a student learns more and more complicated *kata.* But more importantly, he must perform even the relatively simple ones with better focus and concentration.

Practice of *kata* constitutes another important segment of each training session. Repetition of a technique, as explained above, provides one kind of training, but the movements are usually done while first advancing a number of steps in one direction and then retreating in the opposite. In *kata,* on the other hand, the student learns to relate to all directions. From the standpoint of developing proficiency in karate, *kata* comes closer than any other training to actual sparring with an opponent. Thus, in the absence of an opponent, the practice of *kata* enables each student to sharpen his skill.

Students of tai chi chuan attach great importance to the correct performance of a sequential form that requires anywhere from five to twenty minutes to complete. The variation in the length of time necessary to complete this form depends upon the particular style in question. Some teachers teach a "short" and a "long" form, others only a "long," and still others only a "short." The short Yang form, which is rapidly gaining popularity in this country, is not as brief as it may sound. It contains fewer movements overall and fewer repetitions than the long form and, depending upon speed of execution, takes seven to ten minutes to complete. Students must spend about six months just learning the pattern of the movements it contains, let alone doing them correctly. The form consists of various self-defense movements arranged in sequence and done throughout at the same rate of speed. The movements are often stylized and sometimes only faintly resemble the original fighting technique. The form is done slowly, and the position and movement of every part of the body receive careful attention. Karate techniques, in contrast, are usually performed with much greater speed and less emphasis on exact placement of various parts of the body. In the tai chi form, knees remain bent throughout and the back is held perpendicular to the ground. Again, in contrast to karate *kata* where at the moment of focus the performer simultaneously tenses a large number of muscles, the body remains as relaxed as possible and only the very minimum of strength is used. Naturally, if the arm and shoulder muscles are employed in a movement, they become operative and would feel hard to the touch, as would be true of the leg that supports the body's weight. But if a hand must be raised to solar plexus height, it is unnecessary to tighten all the muscles of the arm

or the torso to accomplish this.

Students of tai chi chuan who want to learn to deal successfully with an opponent must move while fighting in the way they move in the form. Thus, in doing the form, there is great emphasis on a relaxed body with minimum use of strength, bent knees with consequent low center of gravity and attention to detail which contributes to a growth of concentration and sensitivity. Students are expected to spend at least twenty or thirty minutes daily in doing the form. Teachers explain that only through daily practice will the student internalize the correct way of moving. The goal is to practice long enough and hard enough until all of the student's movements throughout the day are done in a manner characteristic of the tai chi form.

The use of individual form practice in the three martial arts briefly described above is not limited to them but is characteristic of all martial arts I have knowledge of. Practitioners use this method of training to help develop the skill necessary for performing the many complicated techniques that comprise the body of their art. Moreover, the ability to attain maximum power in each movement is thought to stem from individual practice. However, more than the development of the skillful and powerful performance of various techniques can result from this kind of training. Those teachers who view their art as a mental as well as a physical discipline think of individual form practice as a means of bringing about those changes in students that are characteristic of some form of meditation.

Meditative Aspects of Individual Form Practice

ONE MAY ASK what is involved in such mental training and why is it pursued? Investigation reveals that over the centuries, both Eastern and Western religious and secular groups have engaged in meditational practices which they variously claimed achieved union with God, enabled them to see life in its wholeness and instilled tranquility. Meditation was seldom the province of the mainstream of religious observance in the West but was and is usually pursued by groups inclined toward mysticism. In the Middle East the Sufis and in the Far East the Buddhists, Taoists, Shintoists and Indian

Yogis all depend upon meditation to achieve their particular ends. Members of primitive tribes throughout the world engage in one or another form of meditation for spiritual development. The meditation practiced by all of these groups has certain mental and physical methods in common. Chief among them are muscular relaxation and freeing the mind of everyday thoughts. The intention is to learn to focus the conscious mind on something other than our everyday concerns, which usually receive its exclusive attention. Moreover, students attempt to maintain their focus for longer and longer periods of time, undistracted by intruding thoughts or sensations. This concentration of the mind can be accomplished by repeating a word or a sound, by counting the inhalation or exhalation of the breath or in numerous other ways.

The individual practice of form in martial arts, when it is used as mental training, also relies upon some of the foregoing methods to bring about in its students various changes in the way they view the world. Of course, the light in which a student considers the form, the manner in which he does it and the ultimate outcome of his practice depend in large measure upon the views of his teacher. If his teacher sees nothing more in it than skill-producing practice, progress in this other direction will still occur but will be slow. Despite the occasional failure of their teacher to point the way, students will notice a change in themselves nonetheless. But usually they will be unaware of the potential for development and unable, therefore, to consciously help the process along.

At any rate, a teacher who believes his student should learn concentration through form practice will proceed by asking him to give the form his complete attention. Intrusive thoughts of past or present problems or of intentions concerning the future might rise in his mind, but the student must not entertain them. Ideas unconcerned with the form may appear, but he should ignore them as they come into his awareness and immediately return his attention to the form. He must endeavor to keep his mind on his every movement and try to do it as well as he can. Moreover, he should try to become fully aware of the position of his body and the changing location of its various parts. As he becomes conscious of errors of position or execution in his performance, he must try to determine the reason for his mistakes and try to make the necessary adjustments. This general procedure is more char-

56

acteristic of forms which are performed slowly, but even movements which are ordinarily done with speed can promote such awareness. If speed is too much of a handicap, the form can be slowed down. The drawback in training students to concentrate by the use of forms ordinarily done at a fast pace is that they find it difficult to be fully conscious of what they are doing.

Another facet of individual form training is its emphasis on executing techniques from a low center of gravity. Knees are usually bent in doing a form, but the need for a low center of gravity encompasses more than a superficial lowering of the body. In terms of developing skill, techniques capable of generating maximum power must be done with the whole body. Because the muscles of the legs and hips constitute a large proportion of the body's bulk and form its foundation, or stance, these muscles must be brought fully into play with each movement. Added stability is lent to each technique as the center of gravity is lowered. In addition, even though a punch or a block appears to be done with the arms and shoulders, in reality the main emphasis is on the correct movement of the legs and hips.

Tan tien or Tanden

B EYOND THE apparent lowering of the body and the presence of power in these fighting movements, form practice is designed to effect a more subtle change in the student. This change concerns a gradual sinking or settling of the center of his body, or his conception of his center, to a lower position. This center eventually comes to rest at a point a few inches below the navel. This point is known as the *tan tien* in Chinese or *tanden* in Japanese.

Traditionally, the *tan tien* is a center or reservoir of a form of internal energy which, as discussed earlier, is called *chi* in Chinese. It is considered a point for the nourishment of life. Attempts by adherents of Western scientific medicine to experimentally discover the physiological presence and location of such a center have met with failure. Yet, from ancient times, teachers of mental and spiritual development in Indian, Chinese and Japanese cultures have posited its existence and spoken of the benefits resulting from its cultivation. Teachers of this kind, whose writings are extant or who are presently teaching, base their instruction on the findings resulting from thousands of years of close and careful observation of human beings by their predecessors. Moreover, a teacher of this sort has always been a man with an outstanding grasp of practical psychology and skilled in assessing the extent of human awareness. If such men in different cultures speak of the center of the human body, place it in the same location and cite its importance as a place from which one "acts" and "thinks," then we must attach enough credence to the theory to entertain the possibility that something, in fact, goes on there. All our problems of belief and acceptance clear up, however, when we begin to practice and notice the gradual change in ourselves over the years.

Hara

THE JAPANESE term *hara* seems to include the qualities connected with the kind of centering involved. *Hara* can be translated as stomach, but in the sense used here it indicates the lower abdominal area. In describing a way of functioning that is down to earth, big-hearted and reflective of a broad and deep understanding of human life, the Japanese speak approvingly of a person acting from his *hara* or of having a big *hara*. Beyond the mature way of dealing with life that it immediately signifies, this kind of statement expresses a more fundamental point of view about human relationships and man's place in the world. It implies an acceptance of the idea that we are connected with the world and with one another. We are not separated from the rest of life. The role of the intellect, or the head, in our activities is not ignored or depreciated, but it is understood that intellect must be rooted in those depths of life from which springs all that we do. Without such a base, intellect can become too extreme. Purely intellectual solutions to problems are probably not possible, because other parts of our mind are certain to exert their influence. However, when we attempt to be as rational as possible in our approach, we often become too narrow or restrictive in our assessment of the "relevant" factors that constitute a problem or its solution. We forget that the world is actually an interrelated and intermeshed whole.

It is thought that a person who acts in a way indicative of a developed *hara* walks and moves differently from others. He gives a physically settled and solid appearance, which is not the same as possessing a corpulent or stocky body. For those who are able to judge such things, there is a clear difference in the way people walk and use their bodies. This difference is evident when we compare a person raised in one country, or culture, with a person from another. For example, Japanese would say of most Westerners that they bounce along as they walk, reflecting the high location of the body's center. In contrast, they feel that Japanese generally walk more heavily and somehow are lower in terms of the body's center, expressing a different approach to life from that held in the West. The student of martial arts also begins to look physically more stable and composed as he continues practicing. At first there is no noticeable evidence of any alteration in his usual way of doing things. But it will be helpful for him to believe that the change he seeks is slowly coming about. When it does occur, he may not even be sure anything has happened because it has come so gradually. The clearest indicator he has that something has changed comes when an acquaintance he has not seen for a time remarks on some difference in him. The student may, in his friend's eyes, hold himself and do things in a more composed manner, partly the result of the center of his body gradually dropping. In those persons correctly trained for some years in a martial art or in some form of meditation, be they Eastern or Western, a settled, composed and tranquil way of doing things is evident.

Analytical and Intuitive Aspects of the Mind

As WE LEARN to concentrate, to physically settle the body and to relax those muscles that are unnecessary for doing a technique, we gradually quiet the analytical, reasoning portion of the mind. Why would this be useful or necessary? In our Western culture, we generally react to the world in a rational manner, often distrusting or thinking of little value a more intuitive approach to our problems. Our Western way of viewing the world lends itself to separating out components of a whole in order to examine them more closely, sometimes forgetting that it is the working of the whole

59

that is important. To try to see things in their totality, as they really are, seems essential to our welfare. Tampering with one or another element of our environment without enough consideration for the effect of such tampering on the whole could lead to calamity in some form or other. In a more personal sense, sometimes a too rational approach to life results in failure to see any connection between our well-being and interests and that of other human beings and other forms of life. Our relations with other life might then become exploitive, causing unhappiness and discontent and perhaps bringing some form of retribution in its wake as the exploited attempt to right the balance.

If we recognize the value of approaching life from an intuitive as well as a rational standpoint, how can we effect such a change in our thinking? To begin with, we must first give ourselves a rest from our usual way of viewing the world. Those of us who live in our fast-paced, crowded and noisy cities receive a constant bombardment of impressions from our environment. There is usually so much going on that we are in a perpetual state of distraction, unable to concentrate and often unclear about who and what we are. To preserve our sanity we sometimes shut out or ignore many of the impressions clamoring for our attention. We certainly cannot consciously register every impression made upon us by the world around us. Unfortunately, it is probable that this kind of selectivity also results in our failure to see things as they really are. We usually construct some kind of a mental image that represents the people or things most familiar to us or that we deal with all the time. We no longer see a person as clearly or as vividly after meeting him two or three times. For example, the first time we meet a person or witness an event we bring all our faculties to bear in an effort to assess this new experience. In succeeding meetings, we actually see less or lose the freshness of the first meeting because we have usually catalogued the impressions we received at the beginning. Thus, if an acquaintance has shaved a mustache or beard, we may not even notice this difference in his appearance because we have mentally classified him in a certain way.

The phenomenon of failing to see the uniqueness of each person is also related to this tendency. We usually categorize the people we meet or see around us. If a person says he is a student, the attributes of that occupation spring to mind and he is pigeonholed. A man engaged in some form of

60

manual labor concerned with the erection of buildings is labeled "construction worker" and takes on the various characteristics we associate with that term. However, the people we meet may not fit the mold we have prepared for them in our minds. The ability to generalize in this way has its uses in our culture, but we often forget that the term "teacher" or "student" or "city dweller" includes a vast range of people, many of whom act in ways that might not fit our mental image of them.

To react to life in this way removes much of the freshness that could be a part of everyday experience. It contributes to boredom. Our awareness becomes limited to dealing with abstractions and we miss what is going on around us. Concentrating on the movements of a form in our training gives us a kind of rest from our accustomed way of dealing with life. We have to focus fully for a time on something real and concrete, something we are not allowing ourselves to form a mental image of. The result, over time, of this change in our way of relating to what we are doing is that when we return our attention to outside concerns, we see things more vividly, as if they were fresh experiences. Moreover, a new perspective results from this focus of our attention. Often, too, a different sense of proportion emerges with reduced use of abstract thinking. Personal problems that seemed overwhelming become easier to solve. Seen in relation to the larger issues of life, our problems are reduced to more easily manageable dimensions.

We seem to be concerned here with the way we apprehend the world which we help form and with which we interact. Some of us seem to try to relate to life logically and analytically, while others favor an approach based on emotion, feeling and intuition, and perhaps a denial of the primary importance of logic in many areas. Obviously, it is not a question of the exclusive use of one mode of relating or the other, because everyone constantly combines the two in differing proportions. However, observers of human behavior have remarked on a general tendency on the part of most of us to favor either one or the other.

In the West, it seems clear that the logical and analytical has been considered superior to the intuitive, especially over the last two hundred years. For the past generation or two, literature and movies have often contrasted a dominant male way of reasoning with the weaker female, more sensitive method to the solution of a problem. If a point is at issue, the woman is generally portrayed as having a certain "feeling" about it and lacking the ability to present a cogently reasoned argument in favor of her feeling. As a result of this inability to support the product of her intuition with acceptable reasons, the "feeling" is rejected by the male decision-maker. In this same fictionalized treatment, the woman's apprehensions prove to have been well founded and failing to heed them results in some form of disaster. This presentation by writers and our acceptance of it in that form is a recognition that the dominant logical, analytical approach to the problems of life is fallible, especially when it is employed exclusively, and that there is something to be said for using the mind in other ways. Nevertheless, it is usual for the intuitive manner of relating to get short shrift from decision-makers, unless the insightful flash can be translated into a logical, sequential presentation. Women who cannot reason or refuse to are usually considered scatterbrained. An intuitive means of dealing with life is also thought common to artists, poets and members of some esoteric groups. Although the work done by many people of this kind is considered useful and even valuable to society, they have often been viewed as eccentric and sometimes even dangerous to social stability. This attitude is probably held because the work of these persons usually reflects ideas which are different from currently accepted ones. These ideas are considered irrelevant and perhaps threatening by the great majority during the lifetime of many artists and others with the ability to bring the world into clearer focus. In societies that exercise considerable control over the individual, such persons are subject to censorship lest their work present a point of view that runs counter to official dogma.

Those who subscribe to the theory that the mind has both a logical and an intuitive side, a theory formulated over the millenia through observations of people's behavior, feel on safer ground when this theory is supported by the results of modern scientific studies. This is especially true in the West, given our predilection for evidence which is verifiable under controlled laboratory conditions. In recent years, psychological and physiological research concerned with the brain has given additional support to the earlier thesis. Robert Ornstein in his book *The Psychology of Consciousness* (W. H. Freeman & Co., San Francisco, 1972, 247 pp.) describes the research that has been done on the way the brain works in right-handed human beings.

He writes:

On the physiological level, it has recently been shown that the two cerebral hemispheres of the cortex are specialized for different modes of information-processing. The left hemisphere operates primarily in a verbal-intellectual and sequential mode, the right hemisphere primarily in a spatial and sequential mode. The "right hemisphere" mode is often devalued by the dominant, verbal intellect . . . . This second mode often appears inelegant, lacking the formal reasoning, linearity, and polish of the intellect. It is more involved in space than in time, more involved in intuition than in logic and language . . . . Since it is nonlinear, this second mode is not involved in the "ordinary" realm of cause and effect which underlies so much of our personal and intellectual life . . . . (p. 225)

Ornstein makes the point that the two ways of dealing with our environment are complementary. But he seems to feel that the balance in our Western society has tipped on the side of functions handled by the left hemisphere of the brain. We are primarily intellectual and need additional attention to an intuitional, holistic approach to our problems. He argues for using both hemispheres in the kind of synthesis that will promote the well-being and perhaps the survival of our world.

The desirability of this synthesis stems from the conception that the logical, analytical portion of the brain can get valuable information from the intuitive portion. Also, the intuitive portion can benefit by having its total apprehension of a situation translated by the logical into language or symbols that can be communicated to other minds. The flash of intuition concerning the solution of a problem must be worked through in step-by-step fashion by the analytical portion of the mind if the solution or its results are to be made available in the physical world.

From another standpoint, we ought to be able to bring into our conscious minds information about ourselves and the world around us gathered by the intuitive portion of the mind. Some think that the intuitive portion contains suppressed ideas and wishes best left alone or unexamined. But to think in this way bars from conscious examination a rich field of our own experience which, like it or not, affects us even if we try to ignore it.

Form training can move the student in this direction. It furthers a quieting of the rational, analytical portion of the mind and allows the right hemisphere of the brain more scope. This process can bring about an opening up of the student's perceptions, heighten his awareness and help him to become conscious of more of the world around him than previously. In his relations with other persons, he might find that he is developing the kind of insight that allows him to sense what is really being thought or felt. Often, verbal statements made by another do not square with the particular feeling he transmits. This does not mean that the verbal expression need be rejected in favor of the intuitive feeling. However, a prudent course would dictate a combination of equal proportions of the two methods of relating to others.

Extensions of a More Intuitive Approach to Life

As THIS SORT of practice exerts its influence, the student may alter his method of viewing and solving the problems of daily life. For example, he might begin to admit the possibility of psychic or clairvoyant ability. He might even visit a psychic when he seeks the solution to an important problem. The outcome of such a consultation need not be a total and unquestioning acceptance of the psychic's words. However, what is said could cause the student to encounter and recognize aspects of the problem and possible solutions that he may have missed in taking a generally logical and rational approach.

Increased recognition of the existence and usefulness of mind processes that were earlier thought fantasy or of limited use might turn the student toward such methods of divination as the *I Ching*. The *I Ching*, or Book of Changes, is a three-thousand-year-old book of Chinese wisdom. It is often used as a book of oracles, but can be seen to go far beyond this usage when we learn that it provided a source for both Taoist and Confucian philosophy. At any rate, consulting the *I Ching* when faced with the need for a decision on some difficult subject can help the student toward greater insight. Jung, in his foreword to the *I Ching*, states that the mode of divination to which the *I Ching* is put aims at self-knowledge (p. XXXIV, Wilhelm/Baynes,

The I Ching, Bollingen Series XIX, Princeton University Press, 1950, 740 pp.). It seems to do this by allowing the student to become conscious of his previously unconscious thoughts concerning the question he has asked. The questioning process causes the student to meditate on his problem. The particular answer he gets is not always clear, especially since it is couched in somewhat quaint and poetical language. However, in his attempt to make "sense" of the answer, the student finds that ideas and thoughts that were buried in the deeper levels of his mind begin to come to the surface. He thereby gains new insight into his problem and, usually, into himself as well.

Other members of the occult fraternity, such as astrologers, graphologists and hand analysts, also can help the serious seeker after self-knowledge to see aspects of his character that wishful thinking or inattention might have obscured. Correctly used, such information can be valuable. It can help provide direction and point up those areas in his life to which the student can profitably devote his energies.

Another method the student might begin to employ to gain greater self-knowledge is the analysis of his dreams. Some maintain that they never dream, but such a statement has been disproved by psychologists who study dreaming. Their findings are that we all dream, but that we often fail to remember what we dreamed. They think that this forgetfulness is caused by the conscious mind's censorship of unacceptable desires and thoughts. We do not welcome the appearance of material that fails to support the particular point of view we consciously hold about ourselves or about our relations with others, especially when the new information places us in what we think is an unfavorable light. When we sleep, the activity and strength of the conscious mind is reduced, and these dormant ideas come to the surface. If we try to recall our dreams as soon as we awake we can usually remember their contents. Again as with the *I Ching,* the material may, to our conscious mind, be distorted. Yet important truths concerning our feelings, attitudes and thoughts reveal themselves in our dreams and can be brought into the conscious mind if we make the effort. Once these feelings surface, we can examine them and see ourselves as we really are rather than as we think we would like to be. The direction is once more toward knowing ourselves a little better.

A word of caution should be voiced against the rise of a kind of self-indulgence in our use of various means toward self-understanding. All of us enjoy hearing about ourselves, especially when we receive hope and direction for the future, in the positive terms in which psychics, hand analysts or astrologers are wont to express themselves to clients. (This is not to say persons practicing such arts are not themselves making serious attempts at self-understanding and gaining a clearer perception of the workings of the world. However, they would readily admit that a person who receives a reading is often taking only a faltering first step on this path and that changing the direction of one's life is the work of many years. Moreover, to emphasize negative elements in a client's character or his method of interacting with others might produce in him an unwarranted feeling of the hopelessness of his situation.) Thus, we might run from one occultist to the next in an attempt to get additional favorable information about ourselves, auspicious auguries of the future, or just to have someone devote his attention to our general makeup and our usually unrealized potential. Some of us search avidly for someone who will make an assessment of our character we can accept. We might like to think of ourselves in a particular way and then go from one seer to another, hoping for information that will support our view. This is unrealistic and hinders the growth of self-understanding. Once we begin to know ourselves a little better, some degree of hoping and wishing for some needed or beneficial change is helpful, but it must be supported by disciplined work.

Boredom with our present state of development or our particular life style may also result in a search for titillation possibly provided by an occultist. However, if we can but recognize that each state of development is complete and whole and where we are at the moment, we will be content with it. When changes come, as they must, we should be content with them too, viewing them as way stations along the road we are traveling. Projecting ourselves into the future or into a hoped for personality is to fail to live in the present and again goes contrary to the result aimed at by our martial arts training.

Discipline

FINALLY, doing the form daily helps the student to bring discipline into his life. By "discipline" I mean developing the ability to do something each day which is not always pleasant and about which one is not always enthusiastic. It is easy to engage in some activity which excites us and which we like. However, even though we have made up our minds to live in a certain way, we will encounter many days or perhaps weeks when we are less than eager to do the work connected with our choice. If we practice on only the days we really want to, our progress will be extremely slow. In addition, we are apt to stop our training altogether, because the particular form we are doing becomes easier with daily practice and more difficult when it is done infrequently.

Spending a certain portion of each day in practice, the results of which are not quickly evident, is difficult. Those students who enroll in a school of martial arts which holds daily classes are fortunate, because once the class begins they are swept along in the general procedure. The energy generated by fellow students and the teacher serves to carry each individual along. Those who attend class only once or twice a week and who must practice alone for a period of time each day have a more difficult time of it. At any rate, the general pattern for students is for discipline to be initially imposed from outside themselves. It is true that beginners usually throw themselves into training with enthusiasm. But when this initial flush of enthusiasm begins to fade, they need help in establishing a steady pattern of training. The class situation provides this pattern. Gradually, however, students fall into the habit of training at certain times of the day. If for some reason they are unable to train, they feel that something has been left undone. Once a certain momentum of practice has been established, it becomes easier to do one's prescribed period of training than to avoid it.

This idea of discipline is not a matter of having our mind on the achievement of some future goal. Nor is it tied to the Protestant work ethic. Instead, it stems from our decision to live our lives in a particular way, to follow a certain road. Once we have made such a decision, we must turn our energy as much as possible toward fully doing the things that are a part of our chosen way. When we practice, we must not think we are sacrificing something or suffering in order to attain some reward. The thing we are doing should have been chosen because of its inherent value for us and thus is worth doing for its own sake. Taking the view that we are only practicing in order to get to some imagined goal tends to devalue what is being done. The goal we are striving to reach may not exist or, if we feel we have reached it, may not be at all the way we imagined it. All we really have is our daily practice and living our daily life. The method or the manner in which we live from day to day affects us in a certain way and results in development of one kind or another. We must go on the assumption that undertaking a certain kind of training will put us in a different place five years from now than if this training had not been done. Beyond carefully making our initial selection of a particular road to follow, it is of little worth to speculate constantly about the kind of human being we might become at some future date. The likelihood is that we will not differ very much from the way we are now. Yet even small changes in self-realization and self-understanding are valuable for us.

Attempting to bring discipline into our lives does not call for the avoidance of joy and pleasure. Students will discover that practicing alone or with a partner is often very enjoyable. The relaxed feeling that comes with doing individual form practice is almost always pleasurable. In working with a partner, depending on the martial art, smiles and even laughter are not uncommon. At the conclusion of a free practice period, participants who have put aside their accustomed social facade to reveal more of themselves, as is common in the heat of the encounter, enjoy a warm feeling for one another. Thus, some kind of disciplined training does not negate feelings of pleasure, but may instead even give rise to them.

Still another facet of discipline concerns the necessity for doing something long enough and in concentrated enough fashion to discover what is beneath the surface. Without almost daily and fairly intensive practice in any of the martial arts, we will only experience what is superficial. Of course, any degree of training, even if very mild, brings some benefit. However, if our practice is not intensive over a period of years, we will fail to come upon those elements which only appear at this particular depth. This idea is clearly illustrated in the development of skill. Those persons who train daily for a number of years reach levels of skill that seem impossible to achieve to those unable or unwilling to devote themselves as fully to training. Similarly, in the area of self-realization and self-development, levels are reached with intensive and continuous training that the dilettante can only guess at.

CHAPTER IV

The Result of Training with a Partner

Developing Skill

TO BECOME proficient in whatever martial art he is studying, the student must practice with a partner. In judo, falling and throwing techniques, which at first are learned without an opponent, must soon be done in a more realistic way. Judo on the ground, or grappling on the mat, cannot be learned without someone to hold or from whom to escape. In the various forms of hard-style boxing, a student's form might appear attractive and effective when he displays it in individual practice, but if he has not worked with actual opponents, the unexpected physical contact may upset his balance and reduce the power of his technique. In tai chi chuan, merely doing the form does not develop the ability to avoid someone's attack. We must practice push-hands over some years if we desire proficiency in attack and defense.

Relating to Others

COMPARED WITH doing the form alone, relating to another person in martial arts, as in life, brings a new dimension into the picture. Earlier we were concerned only with performing techniques against an imaginary opponent. When we are faced with a real opponent, much more than a physical body must be dealt with. Even on the physical level we usually experience difficulty in executing techniques, which seem to go so well in individual practice, against an uncooperative opponent. But beyond the physical, the mental, psychological or spiritual aspect of training with a partner is an important consideration. For example, we may be able to function very well when we work alone but may become upset and perform poorly when we practice with opponents. Perhaps we feel threatened in some way or regard the encounter as a test in which we must prove ourselves. We might dislike physical contact with others or become anxious because of deep-rooted fears about violence or aggressiveness. Considerations of this sort enter whenever we confront another person whose interests are in some way opposed to ours.

The more intimate kind of interaction experienced in martial arts training aside for the moment, whenever we meet another person, we experience the impact of his personality. Some persons seem calm and composed, others nervous. We radiate differing amounts of energy, some individuals appearing vibrant with energy to spare and others functioning at a comparatively low ebb. People often look to others to fulfill certain of their needs. We may not want to play the role another person wishes to assign us. Thus, even if no word is exchanged we automatically form some impression of the kind of person we face and what kinds of reactions we might expect from him.

Perhaps we form our opinion of the other person according to the manner in which his general appearance resembles someone with whom we have had a relationship in the past. If our past experience with the kind of person he appears to be has been gratifying and rewarding, our feeling about him would tend to be favorable and positive. If he looks like someone who has proved unpleasant, we would react negatively. The size of our catalog of types will depend on the extent of our experience with others and on the degree of sensitivity we have achieved.

Those of us who are concerned with outward appearance might feel that proper dress, good grooming, or verbal ability constitute good character. We might then respond favorably to a person exhibiting these characteristics, forgetting that most of us hide behind a certain veneer which we think makes us more acceptable to others. Unless some crisis arises, this veneer is seldom stripped away and many facets of our character remain hidden.

Less visible factors also help form our opinion of others. Indications are that more goes on between people than their conversation alone might indicate. We seem constantly to be sending one another messages even if these messages are not verbalized. Some students of human behavior have argued for the existence of a body language in which various parts of the body assume positions which reflect inner feelings. If we accept this theory, we would say that another person's friendly thoughts concerning us are expressed by his body. If we are skillful at reading or understanding such language, we would probably react positively to him. On the other hand, a smiling face or friendly words may be belied by other parts of the body which seem to reflect unfriendliness. In this case, we dislike or distrust the individual, although if pressed we might admit that we have nothing really concrete upon which to base our negative impression.

Even though we are warned by psychologists against judging a person's character on the basis of his appearance and the exchange of a few words, our tendency is to make such judgments and, as cited earlier, to categorize everyone we meet. We may not make judgments consciously but form an impression which, if we find it necessary, would be expressed in the verbal symbols we think appropriate. Of course, our first impression usually undergoes revision as additional information about the person comes to our awareness. When we have dealings of one sort or another with people over time, if we are moderately sensitive we notice what they do and listen to what they have to say. Our assessment of what we might expect of them in various circumstances usually undergoes some degree of change. This method of learning about others usually takes considerable time and the outcome is seldom as clear as we might wish. Moreover, once we have categorized a person we change our opinion of him only with great difficulty.

The ability to assess character varies from individual to individual. Some can see quickly and clearly where another person stands, what motivates him and what he thinks is important. They may have inherited this ability or in some way learned to hear another's unspoken thoughts. Others are not very adept at this kind of appraisal and are apt to be misled by surface appearance. Those without this ability would see others much more clearly if they had an opportunity to observe them in situations where their true selves emerge. Such a situation arises in martial arts training when persons of opposing interests confront one another.

Assessing Character

IN PRACTICE with a partner, the exchange of attitude and intention that normally takes place between people somehow intensifies. This heightened intensity is probably the result of a number of factors. Because this exchange is nonverbal, we are less inclined to allow verbal statements of intention to cloud our perceptions. Moreover, the possibility of injury exists as we physically and psychologically confront someone with opposing interests. If we attempt to proceed as if our opponent's interests are not opposed to ours and fail either to defend against his attack or to attack him vigorously enough, our teacher or senior students will make training increasingly unpleasant for us. In addition, even students on our level of development will be reluctant to practice with us because we seem not to be trying. This emphasis on doing one's best creates an atmosphere in which everyone attempts to demonstrate competence or, more importantly, to show that he is throwing himself fully into the endeavor. In our first few years of training, the most obvious way to prove we are working hard and learning the art is by overcoming the opponents we are pitted against. But as additional time passes, we may begin to assign primary value to considerations other than gaining victory over an opponent.

As we practice with our fellow students and face opponents in matches, we notice that a person's character and the way he approaches life are revealed in the way he conducts himself in the training hall. Opportunities to

take unfair advantage are always present. Does the student avail himself of them? Does he give up when additional effort might have prevented his defeat? Does he seem determined to press home his attack? Does he avoid opponents who are stronger or more skillful than he? Is he careful to avoid hurting those weaker or less skillful than he? When his skill is clearly superior, does he seem to respect his opponent or does he display arrogance? Does he come to practice regularly and on time, and does he practice diligently when he is there? When his defense fails and the opponent's attack succeeds, does he look for an opportunity to engage in verbal explanation or argument instead of dealing with his loss on the level at which it occurred? If he is hurt, does he attempt to carry on if possible?

Additional considerations of a slightly different nature are: How does the student combine technique with power? Does he favor one over the other and, if he does, which predominates? Does he vary his attack or use only one technique? Does he favor roughness over finesse in his overall approach, intentionally inflicting pain on his opponent when he finds the opportunity? Does the opponent's safety seem more important to him than winning?

These questions and others like them might not occur to students as they practice with one another, or they may not be clearly stated. Nevertheless, an opponent's character, or a sense of the kind of person he is, quickly comes through. Because of the way martial arts training is conducted, students are pushed toward total involvement, a situation that gives them little opportunity or inclination to hide their true nature.

Some of this kind of ability to assess others carries over into everyday life. But lacking the kind of confrontation that exists in the training hall, the nature of those persons among whom we live must be determined by less direct, much slower and usually less accurate means. Nevertheless, through the kind of interaction that exists in the training hall we are able to experience at first hand the basic nature of a portion of humanity in the particular culture in which we live. Of course, some selectivity has already taken place in that martial arts training does not appeal to the whole range of personality types within a culture. However, the range is wide enough to afford considerable variation.

Of additional value is the opportunity to spend some months or years practicing a particular martial art in its country of origin. Even though the martial art is the same one practiced at home, with the particular philosophical principles and the rituals that are a part of the art, the student will soon notice an atmosphere and a way of doing things markedly unlike that characteristic of his own country. Few better ways exist to experience cultural differences and to gain a perspective that allows a clearer view of his own cultural background and biases.

Not only does the student discover important and basic information about his opponents when he practices with them, but he learns more about himself. All the questions that were asked about an opponent's behavior under the stress of training can be asked of himself. In addition, he can go a step further and attempt to bring into his consciousness the reasons for his particular way of doing things. He might be surprised to find that he must win at almost any cost. He may not have been aware of this aspect of his nature. If he is interested, he might pursue the matter further in terms of determining the origins of this impulse and its ramifications in his daily life. Another student might discover that confrontation with others makes him anxious and that he favors a passive role and whenever possible avoids any interaction that resembles fighting. Such a person might feel content to practice the individual form but would only reluctantly engage in practice with an opponent. Again, this student might do well to attempt to probe deeper for the causes of his particular behavior.

Competition

IT MAY PROVE instructive to pursue the issue of competition in greater depth, because when opponents confront one another, as they must in martial arts, the whole range of responses resulting from this sort of interaction becomes apparent. Because Asian martial arts spring from a different culture than ours, we would expect ideas about competition expressed or held by teachers of such arts to vary somewhat from our own. It should then come as no surprise when we are told we must try to overcome ourselves, not our opponents. This suggestion is not meant in the sense of defeating ourselves. Rather it concerns seeing our nature more clearly and exercising control over aspects of ourselves which, given free rein, may be thought of as unnecessary burdens on the way along our chosen path. Some teachers say the thought of victory or defeat should not concern us. They also hold we are helping our opponent perfect himself mentally and physically as we do our utmost to successfully complete an offensive or defensive technique. As students gain experience and become older and, hopefully, more mature, they begin to understand the meaning behind these concepts and to grant their validity. However, it is the rare student who in his first few years of training pays more than lip service to these ideals. This is especially true when students are part of a highly competitive culture and when the martial art they practice is sport-oriented.

In our culture, people sometimes experience rather extreme negative reactions to the thought or the experience of engaging in any sort of contest. Generally speaking, however, reactions to competition tend to vary according to how much is at stake. If the outcome means little, most of us can enjoy taking part in some game or contest and are relatively unconcerned with gaining victory or suffering defeat. An example of such a situation might be a game of cards played for small stakes or any game in which our image of ourselves is not threatened.

However, if something more important is in the balance, we are less than eager to pit ourselves against an opponent. If a game seems to depend on the quality of our intellect or some other mental or physical attribute we may hold dear, we become concerned with making a good showing. We are then reluctant to lose. In fact, many of us try to avoid such contests if we stand only an even chance of winning.

It is true that some enjoy any kind of competition, feeling it brings out the best in them. They like the excitement of matching their skill, whether mental or physical, against that of others. Victory or defeat is of secondary importance to the thrill of participation. However, these individuals are rare.

Many of us are not averse to taking part in a contest if we are sure we possess far greater ability than our opponent. We may even use our superior ability to humiliate an opponent. For some of us this method of establishing dominance over another may include hurting him physically if the contest involves physical contact. Naturally, if we envision being on the receiving end of such a proposition we will certainly be reluctant to participate.

The sometimes harsh aspects of rivalry may be thought limited to those games or sports that feature individual performance. Team sports are considered useful for learning cooperation toward a common end or in a common enterprise. In these circumstances, we may be spared the rougher or sterner elements found in direct confrontation. To a great extent, we might be able to depend on our teammates to support us or to extricate us from a difficult position. But even under these conditions, we must often face a direct one-to-one encounter with our opposite number on the opposing team. Also, winning is still the ultimate object. Players usually want to be part of a winning team. If a player performs inadequately he will lose his place on the team to someone who can do a better job. In addition, we should not forget that coaches of losing teams are usually fired.

It seems fairly evident that the manner in which we play games and our reactions to playing are very similar to the way we conduct our lives in the "real" world. We have been taught from our early years that success in life comes through overcoming or defeating others. We are all urged to win rather than to lose. Usually we try to insulate ourselves from the pressure we might feel if we thought our future depended on constant victory. We do this partly by avoiding direct confrontation with someone of opposing interests. Also we attempt compromise where this is possible. Because our economic system usually requires group rather than individual enterprise, we find some degree of shelter from the harshness of direct confrontation by taking a job in which we bear only a small portion of responsibility for the success or failure of the total undertaking. Yet even in these conditions the competitive element is present. To get our job in the first place required some form of competition with others who also wanted it. Within the group, a promotion will often entail competition among fellow workers. Finally, if the company is doing poorly, or "losing," the workers will be told of it and be urged to better their performance on the threat of losing their jobs.

Those who live in this kind of competitive society are generally under a considerable degree of tension. Being able to afford to live what constitutes the good life in our society does not result from suffering defeat or by failing tests of whatever sort. Most of us try to be winners. Unfortunately, where there are winners there must also be losers. For all competitors the possibility of failure exists. For the loser it becomes actuality, but the winner is

also uncertain about the outcome of his next encounter.

This state of affairs seems hard on human beings. Compensations exist, however, for those who can combine hard work with innate ability, inherited wealth or the apparent help of fate. Such persons can be consistent winners. They are rewarded with material benefits and, if they choose, the removal or slackening of the need for competition. In this country, we are fortunate in that even those who experience little success in competition for the bigger prizes are able to get enough to eat and adequate shelter from the elements. Nevertheless, in society's estimation, and usually in their own, members of this latter group are considered failures.

Those who attempt to teach a non-competitive way of relating to others in this kind of culture experience great difficulty. It seems unarguable to most that in daily life winners are rewarded by material comfort, power and prestige. In those martial arts systems that award higher grades in periodic tests, winners rise in grade and losers remain behind. In judo and karate, where students are expected to enter tournaments, winning is, at the very least, considered preferable to losing. Exhortations by teachers urging their students to become indifferent to victory or defeat are met with tolerance based on the feeling that teachers are merely acquainting their students with the philosophy of another culture, or stating an ideal that has little practical value. A parallel might occur in students' minds between the espousal of ideals in martial arts and those encountered in conventional religious worship. Actual practice in both cases lies a considerable distance from the ideal.

Despite the problem of some martial arts ideals running counter to the culture, the situation is not without hope. For a number of reasons the times seem propitious for a change, or the beginning of a shift, in the way most of us live our lives. There is growing awareness that the achievement of a high degree of material comfort is not the most desirable goal of man's life. Many find themselves unwilling to pay the price for the getting of things, a price often paid in the coin of anxiety and constant tension. Others are unable to forego or negate their humanity by exhibiting the necessary disregard for those they must overcome or use to further their ambition. Consequently, those who feel this way are searching for an alternative to the generally competitive mode of behavior that prevails in our society.

However, this search for some alternative way of acting, let alone its actual achievement, is extremely difficult. It is not easy to stop functioning in one's culture. We are very much a part of the environment in which we were raised. Even those who feel strongly disaffected with the way things are done in American society are an integral part of that society. In general, were they to go for a period of time to another country with a different way of doing things, they would find how strongly they are tied to the culture in which they grew up. This realization comes, however, only when they must function in the foreign culture as much as possible as do the members of that culture and not merely as visitors or guests. They begin to notice that the foreign culture goes about solving problems in a way they do not favor. The people there may relate to one another in a manner an American may be able to understand but feels emotionally uncomfortable with. At any rate, even if we thought we might want to, most of us find it inconvenient to drop out or to move to another seemingly more compatible society.

If we are resigned to living our lives in the culture in which we grew up and of which we are a part, we need not think bringing about some degree of change in that culture is hopeless. All of us, to some extent, exert some influence over the way things are done. To some degree, perhaps infinitesimal in many cases, we are capable of affecting the course of events. For example, if we decide that certain ways of doing things are destructive of human values, we might try to avoid those actions. However, we must be able to determine in which areas our efforts to make a change will bear fruit. Also, we must know the extent of our resources and be clear about the degree to which we are willing to commit them to bring about a desirable change. If we attempt to resist a force that is overpowering, our personal situation, which is probably our primary concern, will be far worse than if we had borne the discomfort of tolerating a way of doing things that we think could be improved.

To return more directly to the subject of competition, it seems clear that if we believe something important is at stake, we do our best to win. If we have set our sights on achieving the fruits of victory, it is natural to feel disappointed when we lose. But some find themselves in despair or in deep depression when they think they have been defeated in some encounter. If the trough is very low in defeat or the crest very high in victory, or if these reactions are of long duration, we might try to counter such extremes. To experience excessive reactions of this sort does little to preserve our health and well-being. For many, even the anticipation of taking part in a contest they think important produces anxiety. Fears over the ultimate outcome, as well as reactions to victory or defeat, often take much too costly a toll of our mental and physical resources.

Another problem we face in this connection is that most of us are unable to discriminate between important or momentous struggles or contests and relatively minor ones. The former occur rarely, if ever, while the latter are fairly frequent. But mentally and physically, we react to any confrontation with someone of opposing interests in the same manner. Exceptions, of course, occur when we believe we have nothing to lose, in any sense of the word. However, when we think the outcome is important in some way, most of us find ourselves subject to the unpleasant effects that accompany a stressful encounter.

If we cannot avoid competition, how can we deal with it so it does us the least harm? How can we flatten the curves of elation over success or victory and depression over failure or defeat? One way is to logically come to certain realizations which will provide us with a certain equanimity as we interact with others. For example, in martial arts we may notice that almost everyone loses at some time if he continues training. At the top levels of skill, abilities of the various competitors are so similar that the person we defeat one month might beat us the following month. If we were to be shattered by our loss we would probably perform poorly in future meetings. Considerations of this nature can bring us to the realization that we must learn to be unconcerned with the result of contests, or encounters with others, and that what is done is done for its own sake. Perhaps we see that our reaction to life's challenges need not be tied to past victories or defeats. The strength and flexibility of mind and body we find useful are not necessarily achieved by never suffering loss.

From a slightly different angle, we may be impressed by the thought of the interconnectedness of all life, and that what appears to us as opposition on the part of others is of relatively small moment. Other ideas of this nature may attract us and we may, over time, establish and maintain a tranquil and calm inner core despite the outwardly active, even tumultuous, life we must lead.

Unfortunately, the achievement of this desirable state is seldom the result of logical analysis alone. To make it part of ourselves some sort of training is necessary. This training, as it proceeds in martial arts, gradually forms in us habits of mind and gives rise to understandings which move us in desirable directions.

Learning to Concentrate

WHAT ELEMENTS of training with a partner help produce these beneficial results? To begin with, students must learn to give their attention as fully as possible to what they are doing at every moment. When we are completely engaged in the business of the moment, thoughts concerned with past or future events cannot enter our consciousness. Most of us pay insufficient attention to what we are doing. Our minds are usually filled with thoughts of past events or hopes and fears for the future. We should learn to avoid this way of using the mind. It is wasteful of energy. It can make us ill if projections for the future are threaded through with apprehension and anxiety or if disappointment over past events is permitted to depress us in the present. In addition, we should try to taste to the full our real experiences of life, which come in each present moment, instead of diluting them with extraneous thoughts.

This is not to say that we should avoid planning for the future or ignore mistakes we may have made in the past. But seeking the solution to a problem or charting the course of future action is different from entertaining unproductive imaginary thoughts of possible future disasters or dwelling on past failures to the point of depression.

More concretely, in training with a partner it is difficult for our mind to remain on thoughts other than getting out of the way of a punch when that punch has the power to hurt us if it hits. A throw in judo also is potentially dangerous, providing incentive to learn to move our body into a position that will thwart our opponent's attack. If our defense is inadequate and we are thrown into the air, we make every effort to turn our body so that we fall correctly and without injury. Grappling on the mat in judo includes

88

locks that threaten to injure arm and shoulder joints, as well as strangulation techniques that can cause unconsciousness. In tai chi push-hands, the impact of our body as it hits the wall after a strong push is seldom pleasant. Thus, competitiveness aside, we usually do our best to avoid the discomfort caused by a failure to defend successfully against an opponent's attack. This effort to escape possible injury makes us keenly aware of what our opponent is doing. Consequently, our mind is too fully occupied with the considerations of the moment to wander to thoughts concerned with winning or losing, or of anything but the matter at hand.

A student whose primary consideration is to emerge victorious from any encounter attempts to do everything in his power to assure victory. Thus, he tries to achieve the concentration that is considered necessary if he is to win. However, if his preoccupation with winning and losing is too great, these thoughts may enter his mind as he fights, causing a break in concentration and a consequent weakness in his defense. Of course, this break in concentration can occur to anyone if thoughts unconnected with the business of the moment are strong enough to intrude or if what is being done is not considered important enough to warrant full attention. In martial arts, however, the results of such mind-wandering is quickly apparent as the opponent takes advantage of this weakness to deliver a successful attack. Repeated occurrences of this nature bring home clearly to the student that he must keep his mind on what he is doing.

The particular sort of mental concentration described above engages the mind fully in consciously assessing an opponent's actions and seeking appropriate responses. However, this kind of attention is usually only a characteristic of the early years of training. As one becomes more proficient in one's art, the mind does not pay attention to various details of attack and defense. Rather, the mind is free of conscious thought and the body's response to the situation is allowed to develop as it will. One reason for this is that successful action often requires split-second timing which does not permit the use of the relatively slow mental process in which an appropriate response is first selected and them employed. The particular techniques that are used have been broken down and carefully practiced thousands of times. The breakdown of a technique involves attention to the use of each hand and foot, of body inclination and rotation, of balance and of whatever else a teacher considers important. Over the years, a technique is performed in one explosive movement. As he continues to practice, the student learns to sense openings and weaknesses in an opponent's defense. These openings also are split-second opportunities that appear only momentarily and then are gone. The student must accustom himself to deliver his attack as soon as he perceives an opening. If his mind is on any particular aspect of his opponent's movement or even on what technique he will use when an opportunity presents itself, his response to an opening will be too late. A successful response is usually the result of the mind being "empty," or free of ideas about what is going to happen. The student must remain mentally relaxed and alert and then simply react appropriately when the opportunity presents itself.

This sort of ability develops slowly. It comes only with rigorous training over the years. It is spurred by the student's gradual realization that the result of inattention, in terms of physical pain and failure to develop optimumly, is vastly inferior to the suggested method. As his training continues, the student notices a change in the way his mind works. At first this difference is felt only as he engages in the practice of his art. However, as time goes by he begins to experience this different way of focusing on each moment in other areas of his daily life. He allows his mind to move from action to action as he performs his various activities and does not stop to intellectualize at some point, thereby being to some extent absent from succeeding actions. Thus, when a quick response is necessary, time is not lost in useless or dangerous deliberation.

Being able to function in this way also helps us develop a better mix of the unconscious portion of the mind with the conscious portion. That is, as explained in greater detail in Chapter III, we begin to make better use of that vast area of our mind the contents of which usually only come to our consciousness when the analytical, intellectual, rational portion of the mind is relaxed or permitted to rest. In addition, training with a partner, to a greater extent than individual practice, can help students become more insightful and more attuned to the unspoken thoughts and feelings of others. This is not surprising when we consider that this kind of training combines learning to use the mind in a particular way with rather direct and intimate contact with another human being.

Some martial arts attempt to avoid the competitive aspect of training.

They may dispense with a grading or rating system, avoid contests and in practice with a partner attempt to work cooperatively. It is, however, an open question whether this approach is superior to one that recognizes the competitive nature of the general culture and attempts to teach students to retain their inner equilibrium despite their participation in outward competitive action.

In summary, our primary approach to training with a partner must be to work upon ourselves. We have an opportunity to learn to concentrate upon each moment with positive benefits in other areas of our lives. We find that engaging in competition need not disturb us or prevent us from performing to the best of our capability. Our understanding of our opponents broadens and deepens. We learn to deal with, perhaps not always as successfully as we might wish, the various types of opponents confronting us. Gradually we attain an increased ability to interact appropriately with almost any kind of person falling within the broad range encountered in martial arts. Increased self-understanding is another outcome of this training. As we know ourselves better, we can begin to play down tendencies we decide are to be discouraged and strengthen aspects of our makeup that require this treatment.

CHAPTER V

Philosophy: Its Relevance and Application

I N THE EAST, it is not unusual for people to think of the study of a martial art as training for living life. However, martial arts are not unique in affording this kind of training. Dancing, painting and calligraphy, the playing of musical instruments and almost any activity that is pursued in a serious and disciplined way qualified as a means of working toward self-perfection or self-realization. Over the centuries, teachers of all of these disciplines have embraced various aspects of the philosophical systems of China and Japan that seemed to give theoretical coherence to their training. We should remember, however, that these disciplines stress practice and not theory. An illustration of this bent and of the blending of martial action with spiritual development comes to us from the early history of Zen Buddhism and of Chinese boxing. Tradition has it that the legendary Buddhist monk Ta Mo or Bodhidharma on coming to China from India found the monks at the Shaolin Temple in poor physical condition. He felt that this lack prevented them from achieving their full potential in meditation and spiritual growth. In order to strengthen their bodies and ultimately their minds, he instituted a series of martial exercises which he had learned in his youth. This constituted the beginning of Shaolin Temple Kung Fu, a style that became renowned as a fighting art throughout China.

Philosophical Ideas in Martial Arts

AT ANY RATE, relevant ideas from Taoism, Buddhism and Confucianism were incorporated into the philosophy of the martial arts as they developed through the centuries. Of course, these ideas found their way into, and in another sense underlay, everything that was done in the Eastern societies. However, teachers of disciplines such as the martial arts usually attempted to originate training methods that would enable their students to directly apprehend the content or spirit of some of these philosophical concepts. Their intention was to help students understand important truths intuitively, to develop their insight, rather than to have contact with these ideas only intellectually.

Although the emphasis in martial arts is usually on practice rather than philosophical speculation, teachers will sometimes speak of philosophical concepts which underlie their instruction. Also, an examination of the administrative or hierarchical structure and the teaching method of a school readily reveals the presence of various elements of Asian philosophical doctrine. Of course, one art might stress certain ideas more than might another. For example, a martial art like tai chi chuan may place more weight on certain Taoist concepts than might a harder style of boxing. In general, the following six ideas will be present in varying degrees:

Respect for life and Nature. A belief that we are part of Nature and should attempt to live in harmony with it rather than manipulate it to serve our ends alone. In addition, we should learn to cultivate and preserve life and avoid its destruction. More specifically, in training we are taught to avoid injuring our opponent. We are asked to be gentle and helpful to those weaker than ourselves. If we are forced to use our art to defend ourselves or those around us, we should do so with utmost restraint. Our intention should always be to avoid injuring an attacker if a less extreme method of defense will safely turn aside his attack. Unfortunately, such discretion demands a high degree of skill as well as an unusual concern for the welfare of others. If threatened with injury or worse, even a trained martial artist will seldom employ halfway measures to meet an attack once it has actually been launched. Thus, every effort must be made to avoid an attack before it is expressed physically.

Wu wei or non-action. The idea that the various sytems in Nature are interdependent and that the world will function best if we refrain from disturbing one part or another in order to improve the whole. This concept is clearly related to the foregoing one. Action that interferes with Nature's functioning is to be avoided at the risk of incurring disaster. However, action taken in accordance with Nature's course is justified and necessary. In martial arts, this concept might take the form of helping the body to relax by using certain exercises designed to better enable its natural functioning to proceed unimpeded by tension. This might be reflected in training by not resisting an opponent's attack. The use of this tactic theoretically results in the attacker losing his balance because he has overextended in the direction of a target he mistakenly thought was solid. In this way, we use the opponent's strength to defeat him; or it might be said that by attacking he defeats himself. Finally, many of us suffer from a tendency to overdo or to overcommit our strength in order to accomplish some end. Strictures relating to *wu wei* usually concern themselves with this fault.

Moderation and balance. An avoidance of over- or underextension in any direction. Attempting in whatever we do, to go far enough, but also not to go too far. As with *wu wei,* this concept in martial arts might take the form of avoiding the use of an excessive degree of strength or energy in order to accomplish an attacking or defending maneuver. But it also demands the employment of sufficient energy to achieve a desired result.

Education for training character. The idea that the subject matter a student studies and the method by which he is taught are employed primarily to develop his character. The intention of the teacher is first and foremost to turn out superior persons who would be considered "good" or "worthy" in their particular culture. Knowledge of subject matter would be important as well, but would be secondary. In martial arts, many teachers look upon their calling as a method through which they help students bring about beneficial change in themselves. Often such change is thought to take the form of learning to withstand adversity, of not giving in when things are going badly. However, such stoicism is combined with other traits, such as helping the weak, mentioned above, in an effort to produce strong but gentle persons. These teachers are not concerned primarily with training fighters, although their students usually demonstrate considerable ability in this area.

Filial piety and conformity to the social order. The filial piety learned in a family in which children respect and obey their parents, and younger brothers those who are older, is carried over into society in the form of respect for authority and, above all, proper conduct or propriety. This is not a one-way street, however, since those in a superior position also have their obligations to those below them. This pattern in martial arts lends itself to a hierarchical structure in which the teacher stands at the top of a pyramid with senior students on the level below him and beginners at the bottom. A teacher receives the respect and loyalty of his students, in effect taking the role of the father in the "family" formed by the martial arts school. Senior students assume the role of older brothers.

In addition, certain rules of etiquette are strictly observed within the training hall. For example, students might be asked to demonstrate respect for their training by bowing to the practice area as they arrive and when they leave. They might be required to sit in a particular way. Interaction with fellow students and with the teacher might have to follow a prescribed pattern.

Behavior outside the training hall might also be scrutinized to some degree. For instance, unseemly student conduct outside the school, if brought to the teacher's attention, might result in the erring person's expulsion.

Transcendental spirit and enlightenment. The concern here is with spiritual development. Generally speaking, for Chinese philosophers this does not necessitate a retreat from the world. Rather, the external environment, which we experience each day, provides a means to gain insight into the working of the world and man's place in the scheme of things. Another consideration, or perhaps a way of describing this insight, is enlightenment. Esoteric training methods have been used for centuries to help students penetrate beyond the surface appearance of things and events. Various forms of meditation are perhaps the most important of these methods. The martial arts can be taught with primary emphasis on their meditative character. Those martial arts teachers with the requisite skill in this area do what they can to help students penetrate their self-created veil of illusion about themselves and the world.

These thumbnail sketches of philosophical ideas which appear to be present in martial arts training are not exhaustive. They constitute the major emphasis, but they are interwoven with other minor threads of custom and manners which form the variety and richness of the cultures that produced the martial arts. Consistency of ideas may be absent, as, for example, when transcendental Taoist concepts appear to clash with this-worldly Confucianist ones. Yet a culture appears to have little difficulty in reconciling such apparently divergent ideas. The harmonizing, in the overall culture, of opposing philosophies is not uncommon. But in the East, one often finds such harmonizing occurring in the mind of one individual—an operation that appears difficult and even undesirable to Western thinkers trained to regard opposing ideas as mutually exclusive. Thus, a Japanese may observe Shinto, Buddhist and Christian rites without feeling that to embrace one viewpoint precludes the acceptance of portions of another. Perhaps the feeling about this facet of thought is that differing points of view ultimately lead to the same end.

Some of these underlying philosophical ideas are visible in the brief descriptions of school procedures in Chapter II. It might be useful to round out those earlier descriptions with a more detailed picture of the teaching method at a school of martial arts in which elements of Zen Buddhism are present. If we accept the premise that the teacher's intention at such a school is to help his students see themselves and life generally more clearly, we nevertheless may feel that his methods are unnecessarily stern. If our background is of a kind that excludes acquaintance with such methods, we might even regard them as dehumanizing. However, one of the underlying ideas in this kind of training is that if a student is to grow in his understanding of life he must become aware of aspects of himself that seldom come to conscious attention. To get the student to see beyond the surface of things, physical and mental shocks are employed. The teacher's approach can be characterized as an attempt to put students into a position where their usual manner of viewing life becomes subject to self-examination.

Put another way, the dominance of the ego over the student's life is questioned. By "ego" is meant the mental symbol we use to identify ourselves in our thinking. As we live our daily lives, we usually hold certain ideas about ourselves based on memory, forgetting that these ideas are just symbols and not our real nature. We are changing constantly. We are different from what we were five years ago or one year ago. Yet we approach most situations thinking of ourselves as having distinct and fixed qualities of mind and character. We even have fixed ideas about our physical appearance, although these ideas are more likely to change if we attach a fair degree of credence to what we see when we stand before a mirror. Becoming conscious of possessing certain physical and non-physical characteristics seems to occur to most of us at some particular time in our lives. When it happens, we tend to become locked into that cluster of ideas and find it difficult to free ourselves.

The various qualities we think we have, or display, are determined by the memory of our actions in past situations combined with, or tempered by, wishful or fanciful beliefs about ourselves. Unfortunately, both methods of arriving at an idea of our nature are fallible and lead to an inaccurate assessment. Memory is almost always selective. What we recall about a situation usually depends upon what we expected to see at the time and what we chose to remember. Thus, when we think we behaved in a certain way last month or last year, we are usually being selective and interpretative. Our memory of our actions in some past event and our idea of our character or personality based on these actions cannot but be distorted. This distortion is effected both by our limited ability to see and understand what happened at the time it happened and by the action of memory, after the event, which ignores aspects we believe unimportant or blocks out those that are threatening. The second major factor in the construction of our image of ourselves—the wish or desire to display certain characteristics—does have the power to make a change in us. But for this method to make a real difference in our nature, it must be pursued systematically and intensively over time. Merely wishing for some change in ourselves and even believing that the change has occurred is not enough to transform us to any appreciable degree. And it can lead us to believe we possess qualities we lack or that we are something we are not.

It becomes apparent that our image of ourselves is probably not what we are. Moreover, as time goes by, this image often becomes frozen and no longer changes as we change. As we interact with others, we carry this congealed idea of ourselves into each situation. What is happening must somehow conveniently fit this image or the image must be able to fit into what happens. As a consequence, we become unable to react to each situation as if it were fresh and new, which it is. We attempt to make it immediately into something we may have previously encountered and responded to with some degree of success. On the other hand, we may respond to it negatively, believing it resembles other situations in which we have failed or performed inadequately. Either manner of relating to life leaves little room for spontaneity or for being open enough to see what is really happening. It contributes to inflexibility of mind and a reluctance to try something new.

Thinking of ourselves in this way also has the effect of separating us from other persons, other living things and apparently inanimate objects. We consider ourselves, often proudly, as basically different from everyone else and as unique individuals. Although each of us is unique, we are much more the same than we are different. Our differences should not be permitted to alienate us from others or to result in a feeling of aloneness. Unfortunately, there is no doubt that many people in today's urban environment experience an inability to relate adequately to others, and often suffer a sense of estrangement from the rest of life.

A teacher of martial arts who holds such views about the way most people's minds work, and who believes this state of affairs is unhealthy, will begin to help the student to see himself in a different way. To accomplish this he will probably subject the student's ego to constant attack. This offensive proceeds as soon as the beginner enters a class comprised mainly of more experienced students. It is clear that he has placed himself in an inferior position in relation to these more skillful practitioners. He quickly realizes he really knows little about the art he has begun to study. If he has read about it and is able to verbally manipulate the abstractions he feels are involved, his fellow students will give him credit for this only if his ability in the particular art matches his words. In their training, they have become aware that a thought or an idea of a technique merely represents the technique and is not the technique itself. They may not be able to verbalize this concept, but experience has taught them to mistrust words when they begin to be substitutes for action. Unfortunately, the beginner can seldom match word and deed. The consequence is that if he does not keep his pseudo-knowledge to himself, his fellows think of him as only a talker. This situation is especially true of arts in which the competitive element is strong, such as judo and karate. At any rate, intellectualizing about the art being studied is discouraged, and in this atmosphere the beginning student finds he must turn his energies in another direction.

The road along which beginners are guided is one marked by hard practice and discipline. They receive few opportunities to grasp intellectual handles with which to rationalize their training. Mentally comprehending the subject matter is only the first step on the way to learning. The general overriding concept is that the student must internalize what is being taught and must gradually make it part of himself. To that end he is encouraged to perform repetitious movements either alone or with a partner. As is usual with an attempt to learn something new, he feels inadequate. At first, try as he will, he cannot perform the required movements with the correctness, smoothness, relaxation and seeming total absorption that more advanced students or his teacher demonstrate. Any attempt by the beginner to avoid giving his all to his training is discouraged. Depending upon the art, this discouragement might take the form of especially rigorous treatment at the hands of senior students or the teacher. Attempts to compensate for inadequate performance by recourse to some sort of dialogue is usually treated similarly.

Of course, this method of training presupposes that the beginner has decided to accept the discipline required by his study of the art. The student must have faith in his teacher. Looked at in the opposite way, the teacher cannot accept a student's refusal to do things in the prescribed way without severe injury to his whole endeavor. A teacher will usually regard an argumentative student as a person who cannot or will not give up his idea of himself as a certain kind of individual. If matters deteriorate to such a point that a confrontation between student and teacher occurs, the student is usually expelled. If he is permitted to remain, senior students or the teacher help him to understand his error by subjecting him to unusually severe training. This severity is not considered by those administering it as constituting punishment or as an outlet for sadism. Nor should the erring student consider it in that light.

Training for even the most willing student is rigorous and, viewed from a certain perspective, might be termed sadistic. Also, viewed from this perspective it might be thought that anyone who willingly submits to such treatment has more than the usual amount of masochism in his makeup. But more is at stake here than the everyday relationships of people. The rigorous training is not an end in itself. It is designed to enable the student to experience aspects of himself that usually remain hidden, or that he was unable to see because his prevailing idea of himself obscured his views. He is often pushed beyond the limits he would have chosen for himself, finding that he can go far past the point of apparent physical endurance. He learns about his capabilities under this and related kinds of pressures. Usually he begins to see that he is not what he thought he was, and that what he remembers of himself may well have been inaccurate. Ultimately he discovers that he functions from a different base than the idea he has of himself, or his ego. He will begin to find that he can approach a situation more openly, allowing it to develop and reacting spontaneously as the necessity for action presents itself.

Combined with the training methods described in Chapters III and IV, the foregoing approach helps move students toward self-realization. At this point the reader might well ask what is meant by the term "self-realization." Perhaps as a general definition we can say that the person who engages in serious martial arts training for a few years will be helped to more fully realize his potential as a human being. Certainly he will know more clearly who he is. (He will also learn to see his training partners with additional clarity.) He will become aware of the strengths and weaknesses of his character. He will learn that sustained application of energy over a long period is the way to get a job done that seems hopeless of accomplishment at first encounter. Thus, he will gain the strength and discipline necessary to further develop aspects of himself which he believes are beneficial and to restrain those he decides are detrimental to his well-being. Finally, he will learn not to give up even when he appears to be in a losing position. Such lessons are invaluable for living life.

Individual Differences in Students

OF COURSE, students who engage in martial arts training will respond to it in a variety of ways. Differences in personality and outlook cannot but make themselves felt. Most teachers will recognize and make some allowance for individual differences, but deviation from the requirements of the rather severe training cannot be tolerated. If the training is changed to make it more attractive or more palatable for some students, it would become less valuable for others.

It may be of value to dwell at greater length on the matter of individual differences and their handling in martial arts. We all recognize that human beings are similar in their mortality and in their need for those basic elements like food and shelter that keep them alive. In addition, human beings are creatures who seem to function best as members of society, rather than existing alone. This may be true because cooperation between people appears to result in greater economic benefits to everyone concerned, if it is not actually essential to survival. Even if this were not true, there is little question that most of us need interaction with our fellows if our lives are to have meaning or in some sense be moderately satisfying. It is in social interplay that our character traits, however they are formed, are most clearly seen and, in general, their consequences most strongly felt. Perhaps this is so because comparisons between people are most easily made in this area. Although it is highly unusual to encounter a person who exactly fits a particular classification, we usually place people in personality categories which seem broadly to describe them. Thus, we are able to say, for example, that some persons seek to dominate their fellows and some are willing to be led; some seek the limelight and others are retiring; some are forward-looking and others live with little regard for the future; some can make quick decisions and others seem unable to decide anything at all.

It becomes fairly obvious, then, that students who come to martial arts schools to begin training will differ from one another in their mental and physical attributes and capabilities. Their reaction to the training they undergo and its impact upon them will vary depending upon the kind of person they are and, consequently, on their attitude toward it as they practice. Unfortunately, a sizeable number of beginners will give the training little chance to affect them or really get to know what it involves because they will drop out after a few practice sessions or lessons. Some of the students who continue training will be afraid of suffering physical injury. A few will resent their teacher's criticism. Others will enjoy one aspect of training but intensely dislike another. A small number might enjoy bullying or hurting those weaker than themselves. Many other differences between students will also appear. However, the training they undergo is designed for a fairly wide range of personality types and should not exclude anyone falling into the broad category considered "normal" in our society. If a student is unable to overcome his negative feelings about the training, he will leave. It will not be changed to accommodate him.

Those with various reservations about their training who continue to practice despite their problems will find their thinking and attitudes changing. Perhaps they are overcoming some of their fears, or discovering some of what it is their teacher is trying to do. As time goes by, they will experience the impact of the beneficial effects of the various aspects of training described in the foregoing chapters. At any rate, the direction of the change is usually toward the positive. Thus, this kind of training can be of value to almost every type of person who engages in it for a reasonable length of time. Just as almost everyone, no matter what psychological type he may be, can do physical exercise with consequent improvement in health, the various outcomes of martial arts training, summed up as self-realization, can also be of universal benefit.

Those who have had contact with someone who has studied one of the martial arts may disagree with the idea that such training can make one a "better" person. The person they know may not, in their estimation, exhibit exemplary traits. He may even be a ruffian, or enjoy fighting, or demonstrate some character defect. Depending upon the observer's moral convictions, the person being judged may seem to have a somewhat low standard of conduct in his relationships. We must remember, however, that martial arts training varies in content and method from teacher to teacher. The kind of training designed to move students toward self-realization is found less often than training that aims at the acquisition of skill with little regard to other considerations. Even where emphasis is on self-realization, there is no guarantee that the training will, after a given number of years, produce a certain kind of man. If we are to make a valid assessment of the effect of martial arts training on a particular person's character or mental state, we must first know what kind of person he is. More to the point, we must have knowledge of the kind of person he was before he began his training. Only with this information can we attempt to determine how his training has affected him.

A related point concerns the average person's misconceptions about the outcome of training for self-realization. Such training does not appear to confer god-like qualities upon anyone. The term "enlightenment," sometimes used to describe the result of certain kinds of training, is fairly nebulous. Not all cultures define the term in the same way. In my experience it has come to mean the growth of insight, of the ability to see oneself and others and the world more clearly. This process appears to be endless. Moreover, we should not expect to know everything in some final and ultimate way. Achieving such complete knowledge is probably not possible for us, given our imperfect and fallible understanding. We must also remember that human beings are human beings, with a wide range of characteristics, from those that we would associate with animals to those thought to be possessed by saints. We must learn to accept this range of qualities within ourselves. Those who wish to limit their acknowledgment of the qualities they possess only to an inclination to help others or "do good," should not be upset or shattered if they find themselves acting in stressful situations in a way they consider inappropriate or inconsistent with their intended direction. Nor should any of us fall apart mentally if we experience desires which we consider repulsive in human beings. Our thinking about ourselves should be broad enough to accept ourselves as we are.

Difficulty of Meeting Ideals

HOWEVER, let us suppose that we have decided that in order to live life as well as we can we must meet certain standards in all that we do. Those of us who are not too hard on ourselves might expect periodic lapses from the pursuit of or adherence to these standards. In defense of our inability to live fully in accordance with a selected set of moral and ethical considerations, we might decide that such lapses neither negate these considerations nor are inconsistent with our professed leanings. Trying to deal with the reality of our far from perfect adherence to our abstract ideals, we might settle on the

108

usefulness of holding to some middle course in all we do. We would then attempt not to overdo or go to an extreme in any area of life, but would do whatever we undertake in moderation.

The decision to act in moderation may also come from dissatisfaction with the aftermath of overindulgence in pleasurable activity. If such overindulgence regularly brings some degree of pain in its wake, the thoughtful person might decide to exercise some control over the activity. He may attempt to reach the point where the degree or duration of pleasure is somewhat reduced, but resultant pain is minimized or absent. Another example of behavior that might be considered extreme occurs among those of us who work ourselves too hard or discipline ourselves too harshly. At some point, an assessment of our lives might reveal we have gone much too far in the use of a method that seemed to promise an effective and perhaps quick avenue to a desired goal. When we reach our goal, we may decide the reality falls short of our anticipation. But whether or not this occurs, we may discover we have begun to maintain an overly rigid approach to life. In other words, the somewhat extreme means of reaching our goal, which we may have considered only temporary, has become part of us and is making our lives less wholesome than we might wish.

The foregoing experiences can bring us to the conclusion that our lives might proceed more satisfactorily if we attempt to avoid excesses or extremes. We are then faced with the question of what constitutes extreme behavior. We know we must expend enough effort over a long enough period to do what needs doing. But how much effort is too little and how much is too much? At which point in the pursuit of some goal do we decide we are going too far? Except through the uncertain and sometimes dangerous process of trial and error, how do we calculate a middle way?

A partial answer would seem to lie in the development of sensitivity to ourselves, to others and to the various forces in play in a particular situation. Perhaps the correct word for this quality is awareness, the constant attempt to have our antenna up and functioning fully. If we are confronted with a state of affairs which calls for some response or for action on our part, we want as far as possible to perform in a way that will benefit everyone, or, at the least, to do as little harm as possible. To do this, it is helpful to know ourselves and the persons we are concerned with as well as we can and, in general, to know as much as possible about the situation in question. This information will come to us in a variety of ways, not the least among them the exercise of our intuition.

Attempting to steer a middle course in our actions requires another quality. This is good judgment. After getting the maximum information a situation affords, we must be able to determine the most suitable way of proceeding. Such a determination calls for the exercise of reason, but it also requires a feel or sense of the reality of a state of affairs. Experience in living is one way to develop good judgment. Unfortunately, however, many grow older with little appreciable increase in their possession of this quality.

The employment of awareness as well as good judgment is, however, not enough. Another important component of choosing and then holding to a middle way is control, or the ability to direct and regulate our behavior. Even if we are able to ascertain the correct course in some situation, we must be determined enough to follow that course. When it becomes clear that we have not expended sufficient energy to accomplish our ends, we must be strong and persistent enough to press on until the matter is successfully concluded. If our assessment of a particular situation calls for withdrawal, we must possess enough resoluteness to be able to pull away.

The exercise of control is not always easy. If, for example, we sense that all is not as it should be in our relations with another person, we might decide that it would be in our best interests to sever this connection. Whatever degree of awareness and good judgment we possess will have entered into such a decision. Let us also assume that we have included in our calculation the information that comes into our consciousness from the more intuitive portion of our mind. Moreover, our judgment will have been made with all the strength of our reasoning power we can bring to bear. Some might argue that the employment of reason is difficult here because we are often unable to distinguish clearly our motives in pursuing a particular relationship and, in addition, miscalculate the strength of these motives. Let us grant, however, that we are clear about our motives and have given other relevant factors their correct weight in our analysis. We have made the decision that, difficult as it may be, we must withdraw from the relationship. At this point, it is necessary for other elements in our makeup to come into play. If these elements lack sufficient strength, we will find ourselves unable to act on our decision.

If the first part of this process—gathering information, logically analyzing the problem and coming to a decision—is difficult, the second part is no less so.

It seems to most of us that the situations we meet in life, or the state our lives are in, just happen or that we somehow drift into them. We fail to realize that in all likelihood we are responsible for our lives and for what happens to us. Possibly, from a combination of conscious and unconscious motives, we have chosen these situations for ourselves. In order for some part of our nature to better express itself or to develop, we may set ourselves a particular problem. Whether or not we share this view, it seems unarguable that our capacity to work through a problem with the likelihood of achieving a favorable solution increases according to the measure in which we possess the various abilities discussed above. It would seem too that the experience gained from the process of seeking the solution to a problem is of a different quality, or of an enhanced degree of refinement, if the problem is undertaken with the help of these abilities in considerable measure.

Unfortunately, however, individuals who have developed these various abilities to any appreciable extent are not numerous. Awareness, insight, judgment and determination, important elements in holding to an attractive philosophy of life, do not grow in us simply by our hearing of them or thinking them desirable. Intellectually acknowledging their worth is merely the first step in making them part of ourselves. Our behavior in situations is the result of the way we are, not of the way we might wish to be. If we have not internalized those abilities or attributes that allow us to relate to life in a particular manner, our philosophy usually fails to meet the test of untoward events. Thus, we find ourselves time and again taking an extreme position or reacting in an unsatisfactory way. These failures often come when we face a crisis. Some mishap—suffering an accident, the injury of a loved one, or a financial setback—that evokes a strong emotional response frequently shows us that the particular philosophical approach we may have thought during some peaceful moment was ideally suited to our lives does not hold up in times of stress.

The question is then—how can we internalize a particular philosophy? More specifically, how can we develop in ourselves qualities we believe desirable? Personal experience and observation of others seem to indicate very strongly that desirable traits are not easily secured. Many persons thought to be possessed of wisdom, who have written about or taught methods of attaining certain abilities, have advocated some form of mental and physical discipline. Beyond question, the martial arts have been and can be used in this way.

In undertaking such a training method, it becomes not so much a matter of striving to incorporate a certain philosophical outlook in ourselves or of attempting to make desirable qualities of mind a part of us. Rather, training of this nature seems to bring a particular approach to life in its wake, almost as a side effect. As we proceed, our teacher does not say, "Our practice this week will make us more aware of ourselves and others or develop in us better judgment or more determination." Instead, we simply engage in our daily practice, giving whatever we do full attention. Through this method we affect both our body and our mind.

As we do individual exercises and practice together over the years, certain changes occur in the way we move, in the way we hold ourselves and ultimately in the way we think and feel. In essence, a kind of physical and mental calming and settling takes place. From the physical standpoint, we are taught to move from the lower part of our body, bringing the legs and hips into every movement. Related to and reinforcing this emphasis is the attempt, in some martial arts, to develop the *tan tien* (Chapter III). Where the *tan tien* receives special attention, we gradually learn to keep our energy in this lower abdominal area and to direct this energy onto a target when we choose. In addition, all martial arts students are taught to keep their muscles relaxed when not engaged in some action and to use the body and its energy as efficiently as possible. As a consequence, the physical appearance of students with some years of training is usually one of relaxed alertness stemming from the absence of tension and their centered and coordinated way of moving. Contrary to their placid appearance, such persons can move with quickness and certainty in response to a sudden threat. Faced with a physical emergency, a person trained in this way does not have to take the time to think or turn over in his mind a particular answer to some danger. He acts automatically, and usually correctly, bringing his highly developed skills into play.

As pointed out in the foregoing chapters, martial arts training is designed to elicit from every student a total mental and physical commitment and involvement. Thus, as their bodies become relaxed and settled, their minds also, in a manner of speaking, begin to change in this direction. The various aspects of training designed specifically to work upon the mind have their effect. The result, after the passing of some years, is a change toward greater calmness and serenity. Yet mental alertness and awareness are also present. Also, we may use our minds differently than in the past, perhaps allowing the intuitive portion more play and thus getting into closer touch with what we are and what our relations are to the rest of life.

In addition, we will come to know that there is no substitute for our own experience in finding what life is about and deciding how to live it. Over the years, martial arts training provides this essential experience. Moreover, it promotes the growth of awareness which enables us to fathom the content of the experience encountered both inside and outside the training hall. We begin to see that we need not rely upon others to tell us what we are and what we should be thinking or feeling. When we are confronted with the ideas of others in these realms, we are not reduced to weighing conflicting statements on a balance, with truth being on the side where the largest accumulation occurs. Rather, we can test the validity of another's ideas against our own experience and can accept or reject them from this solid ground.

As we live from day to day, all of us face problems of varying magnitude. We do our best, with the equipment we have, to solve them in the most appropriate way. Our training may be said to have added to this equipment or strengthened it by sharpening or enhancing certain desirable qualities of mind. Perhaps the most noteworthy change is the rise of a kind of feeling or sense of how far to go in certain directions. We may also, because of this sense, automatically reject some possibilities. Where the application of effort, persistence and determination are deemed necessary, we find these qualities to have formed in us. It is as if a kind of regulator grows in our system that works to keep us from going too far, exercises restraint, but allows us to react appropriately when quick or sustained effort becomes necessary. Action taken from this particular ground is felt to be right and is generally not subject to reservation. When faced with a crisis, we need not review our philosophical outlook, if we consciously have one, searching for the correct course of action based on abstractions which we probably have not internalized. Thus, we can act in a more unified way, perhaps even spontaneously. Nor need we force ourselves, where this is even possible, to take action which seems logical but which we somehow sense is inappropriate. Above all, we find that our judgment or decision is usually sound and seems to stand the test of time.

We must remember, however, that no matter what training he undergoes no human being fully possesses these attributes. For most of us it is a question of slow and halting progress on this path, with death cutting short our movement before we have advanced very far. Yet even to have advanced a little way along this road is preferable to not having started at all.

CHAPTER VI

Problems Encountered at the Outset of Training

I N THEIR first year or two of training, students of martial arts often find themselves drawn to, or favoring, one particular aspect of the discipline they are studying. This attraction might be there even before they begin training or it could develop over time as the various facets of their discipline come into focus. As an example, a beginner might feel that the physical exercise he must do is of special value. He might have begun his study because the muscles of his body no longer have the tone they had in earlier years or because his health is not all it should be. Of course, as he practices over the weeks and months, he senses that his training encompasses far more than the physical exercise he wants and needs.

For instance, as he gains some proficiency in his art, he may notice a growth of self-confidence. This change, as well as specific aspects of his training, may help him to relax both physically and mentally. The tense muscles which caused him discomfort in the past may lose some of their rigidity. He may begin to find that the mental stress he encounters in daily life no longer incapacitates him and may even serve as a stimulus to constructive action. Another result may be a greater awareness of the state of his body and a growth in the ability to hear the messages it sends him concerning its needs. As he trains with others, he begins to know more clearly how he behaves when confronting someone with opposing interests. Finally, if his teacher is so inclined, the student will being to view his training as a meditation and know that he is developing mentally in ways that will ultimately affect his life in a positive way. But even after noticing that the art he is studying is really multifaceted, the person in question may continue to regard his practice essentially as physical exercise.

Another person may, at the outset, view his training as primarily enabling him to defend himself from physical attack. He too will engage in all aspects of training and become aware of the benefits that exercise and meditation provide. But he will think of the physical exercise he does as a way to strengthen his body and consequently make his movements faster and more powerful. The various *kata*, or individual form practice, he is asked to do will be regarded largely as a way to improve his technique. He will notice that the practice of *kata* helps him to achieve better balance and timing and enables him to use his body in a more unified way, bringing an increasingly greater amount of his potential power to bear in a given instant. However, he might do the very minimum of *kata* in the belief that free practice with an opponent will more quickly enable him to develop his fighting skills.

Still another person may feel that for him the essence of martial arts involves gaining additional insight into his own nature and its relationship to the rest of creation. He thinks of the mind and body training he undergoes as increasing his capacity for awareness and attention—sharpening the tools he needs in his attempt to apprehend reality. He might believe that Buddhist or Taoist philosophical principles are expressed physically in the martial arts. His training would then constitute a way for him to better understand and perhaps internalize this view of life.

In this latter sphere, a student often encounters rather formidable problems concerned with his understanding of what is being taught. But these problems are also present in aspects of martial arts that, in our Western sense, are largely of a physical nature. If, for instance, only the use of the body seems to be in question, it is natural for beginners to believe they know what their teacher is asking them to do and that with a bit of practice they can soon begin to perform creditably. They would be very discouraged if they thought they were unable to understand their teacher's idea.

Let us pursue this line of thought by examining the concept of the optimum use of physical strength in martial arts. In a soft or internal style of boxing like tai chi chuan, the use of outward physical strength is discouraged in favor of the development of an internal power. It is felt that emphasis on the external will impede the growth of the internal. In harder styles of boxing, or in arts that are concerned with throwing and grappling, external or muscular strength is favored. But strength is used judiciously, at chosen moments. The body is not in a constant state of tension. Students are exhorted, in the harder styles, to stay relaxed and to conserve their energy. To illustrate this point, it is not uncommon for young and strong judo players who have an opportunity to practice with very experienced, and perhaps quite old, judo men to find themselves handled with ease. The old men have learned to neutralize their opponents' power and to use their own strength in a way that make their movements seem effortless.

When the idea of using their strength in this optimum way is described to students, they usually think they understand what is meant. As they attempt to put it into practice, however, they become aware of a considerable gap between what they want to do, or think they want to do, and what their body is actually doing. Of course, it is the teacher's or the senior student's judgment that is accepted as the criterion. Thus, what might seem a correct use of strength to a beginner is usually far too tense or too strong in the teacher's estimation. A very few students go in the opposite direction, using almost no strength at all, causing their movements to be flaccid and of no substance. Embarking on this latter course is more likely to occur in systems like tai chi chaun. It is rather uncommon in harder styles of boxing, because a strong punch or kick will crash through an insubstantial block. Also, the employment of too little strength seldom occurs in arts that are concerned with throwing and grappling, because beginners attempting this method usually find themselves unable to attack or defend with any effectiveness.

Sometimes a student will intentionally refuse to put his teacher's directions into practice. He will not overtly defy the teacher, but may consider his own judgment superior to anyone else's and fail to accept a teacher's criticism and guidance. He may then go his own way, satisfied he is practicing correctly. He will usually judge his progress by the results he gets in competition with other students. As long as he appears to be winning, he will think his method is right and eventually perhaps even believe his interpretation of the teacher's prescription is the proper one. Such a situation can easily occur where a physically strong beginner enjoys an initial advantage over his opponents. Because he is successful in overpowering his fellow students, he may continue to concentrate on the development and use of strength.

As time passes and his fellow students become more skillful, the strength factor becomes less significant. Opponents begin to demonstrate an ability to neutralize his strength. He may then begin to realize he is on an incorrect course. However, he may have accumulated too big a stake in his earlier method to allow him to change. If he is unable to change, he may begin to avoid practice or spend additional time on strength exercises in the hope that he will be able to offset the growing skill of his opponents.

Fortunately, not many are so strong that it will cause them the kind of difficulty mentioned above. Moreover, for strength to become a problem it must be combined with an unwillingness or inability to follow the teacher's direction.

A situation which further serves to blur the clarity of a beginner's idea about the use of strength is that most lack the muscular development necessary for the crisp and decisive movements necessary in martial arts. Their legs, especially, are usually too weak at the outset. The need to strengthen the body serves to complicate a beginner's attempt to exercise discrimination in his use of power. It is somewhat confusing to be told to get stronger but to use this strength only at certain times or in a particular way.

As practice continues, students begin to realize that it is difficult to use strength in an optimum way because much more than the use of strength is involved. Students find they must develop other abilities which combine with strength to enable them to attack and defend with maximum effectiveness. For example, it is important for them to become sensitive to the state of their body. They must know if their muscles are tense or relaxed. They must heighten awareness of the body's actions from moment to moment. Also, the slightest changes in an opponent's position, or even his attitude, must register themselves in the student's mind. If such a change signifies the start of an attack and he is late in noticing it, the student's counter will probably be overly extreme or may fail completely. He may have to compensate for his failure to sense change soon enough by using more strength to respond than would have been necessary a split second earlier. Also, the tension in the body resulting from a tardy response to an opponent's initial attack makes it even more difficult to react correctly to a second or third attack. These considerations might all come under the heading of good

118

timing, or moving at the moment an opponent is most vulnerable.

A student might also have compensated for his inability to notice a change in the situation soon enough by attempting to increase the speed of his response. But to increase reaction time is difficult under conditions where techniques are performed in split seconds. Moreover, this possibility is beside the point in the present discussion and is also subject to the criticism that it is an attempt to make up for inattention or lack of sensitivity.

Beginners are, then, unaware of the complexity of an apparently simple concept or its interrelatedness with these other attributes or accomplishments. In trying to use their strength correctly, they are handicapped because their sensitivity, their feel of the situation, is relatively undeveloped. Naturally, it is not expected that this kind of clarity is present in students when they begin their training. Yet, ultimately it must come if students are to derive from their training the psychological benefits it offers. The misuse of strength hinders the growth of the kind of sensitivity in question.

Another hindrance to the development of this sensitivity arises because beginners are almost always mentally anxious and physically tense. They are embarking on an activity that is unfamiliar and capable of producing physical injury. But they are usually unable to notice this tension in themselves or, if they are aware of it, think it normal. Teachers who recognize this problem emphasize relaxation, and the release of tension. They may suggest a minimal use of strength in order that the kind of sensitivity mentioned above can develop.

To some extent, as beginners continue practicing, the growth of familiarity with what they are doing relieves anxiety and physical tension. The time factor is very important in the rise of a student's ability to understand what appear to be elementary concepts. Without the requisite experience in martial arts training, it is doubtful if a beginner fully grasps the ideas his teacher tries to express through language. It often happens that a student who continues to train for a number of years suddenly perceives the reasoning behind a particular way of doing things. Also, he might have been told to do something in a certain way and thought he was doing it, only to find, after a year or two, that he had not really understood what was required.

It would appear, then, that concepts which are considered easy to grasp by beginners lacking experience in this physical area are in fact rather elusive.

A better understanding only comes with the passage of years spent practicing and the accumulation of experience. If we switch our focus to concepts considered more abstract, we are confronted with the same problem, but perhaps to an even greater degree. For example, the ideas of self-realization or enlightenment are often treated by teachers and students as if one could grasp their essentials by talking about them. However, many teachers have pointed out that the word is not the thing. Words are only the labels we attach to some part of our experience and are not the actual experience. They are meant to represent reality but can do so only in a limited way. In the kind of training found in martial arts, words are a poor substitute for direct experience. Lacking the particular experience, a student will have only a vague idea of the meaning of a teacher's words. As he practices over the months and years, the words a student thought he "understood" at the outset are then filled with additional import, usually somewhat closer to the teacher's intention. With the passage of more years of training, still deeper layers of meaning may reveal themselves.

Mind Control

IT MAY BE well at this point to sound a cautionary note concerning the use of the mind as an instrument to bring about changes in our lives and fortunes. Students may have read about or heard of the possibility of changing their lives in some way simply by wishing for it. A brief, and perhaps less than just, description of this method has us proceed by imagining or visualizing a desired state of affairs as already present in ourselves. With the conscious portion of the mind we order the unconscious portion to work in ways that will bring about the desired results. Such work goes on over time, especially if what is desired constitutes a change of some magnitude. It is felt that the situation the conscious mind visualizes comes into existence on a mental plane and then gradually becomes evident in daily life.

This method is not a game in the sense that the something desired is frivolous or mere whim. The practitioner should know what he is about and must be clear in his choice of direction. In our lives, we all seem to use

this method to some extent. But we usually fail to bring into play the necessary intensity, the focus on a specific objective or the persistence over time.

To use this method in attempting to become skillful at a martial art is probably helpful in the sense that we should try to achieve our ends with all the mental and physical energy we command. But it soon becomes clear to the student that working only mentally to become skillful produces proficiency of a relatively low order. In learning a skill, hopes and wishes are inadequate substitutes for practice.

However, in the area of self-realization, using the mind in the manner described appears at first glance to hold some promise. Yet in this area too, a difficulty presents itself. If the reasoning presented earlier in this chapter is accepted, then it is probably true that a person is uncertain or unclear about what it is he desires until after he has developed to a particular degree. He must himself have experienced what can only be inadequately expressed through verbal symbols. Thus, a beginner can know only in very general terms what it is he wants from martial arts training. He probably feels an attraction, or yearning, for some state of mind which he believes will be more satisfying than his present one. But the particular idea he has about what can be achieved may be incorrect and get in the way of solid progress. It could cause him to look far afield for what may be close at hand. If the idea he has of a desirable mental state is based on inadequate or incomplete knowledge, attempting to change his life to correspond with this probably confused idea will hinder rather than speed development.

Selecting a Teacher

THE DISCUSSION at the beginning of this chapter concerned a student's preference in his training and proceeded from the standpoint that a choice of martial art and teacher had already been made. It is often the case, however, that a person's choice of martial art or of his teacher depends upon what he is looking for. If he wants to learn self-defense, he will try to find a teacher who can help him toward his goal. If he is concerned about his health and wants to exercise, he will have little trouble locating a place to practice. However, if he seeks training that will help him develop beyond the apparent, surface appearance of martial arts, he will have to find a teacher who is capable of pointing him in this direction. Moreover, the teacher must view this aspect of training as his primary task. Such teachers are available, but they are not plentiful.

In general, teachers in their early years seem mainly concerned with producing students who can demonstrate physical skills or, if the martial art is sport-oriented, the ability to do well in contests. Beyond exercising the outward discipline characteristic of the traditional manner of teaching in the particular system, there is little concern with other aspects of a student's development. Teachers of martial arts who consider themselves engaged in something more than the teaching of a skill are usually older and possess a few decades of practice and teaching experience.

How can a beginner find a teacher of this sort? One method is for him to visit various schools in his area in order to observe the classes in session. As he watches, he will begin to get certain impressions from the interaction of teacher with student and of student with student. For example, some schools will reflect a quiet, settled atmosphere, while others will seem noisy and boisterous. In some he will notice a careful and systematic method of teaching, while in others instruction will appear haphazard and incoherent. As he observes the teacher at his work, the beginner will notice the kind of man he seems to be. The teacher should embody, in some measure, the settled, centered, mature way of dealing with life the student might be drawn to. Of course, he is observing the teacher on his home ground where he controls the proceedings and where he enjoys almost every advantage in any exchange with his students. Moreover, students are there because they want to learn what he has to teach and are not persons with interests opposed to his. Nevertheless, the beginner will probably form some sort of judgment concerning the teacher's ability, his quality as a human being and, most important, his desirability as a teacher.

Although the foregoing method of choosing a teacher can provide useful information, success in finding the right teacher by this means requires an observer of rare discernment. He must be able to see beneath surface appearance. Some teachers act out a role and ultimately are not what they seem. An atmosphere may appear serious because teacher and students are

124

merely following the outer form of some esoteric tradition. The observer may fail to notice the lack of real substance in the training. Or the observer himself may suffer from certain handicaps which interfere with his judging ability. For example, he may suffer from an inability to accept criticism and thus would avoid a school where he felt the teacher would tell him of his mistakes with insufficient regard for his feelings. In another instance, the beginner might consider the kind of discipline maintained in a martial arts class distasteful. He might then reject a school in which the teaching appears contrary to his views concerning polite interaction between persons in his society, perhaps to his loss. Also, if he is not sure what the teacher is attempting to accomplish, he will be unable to make more than a superficial judgment about the efficacy of the teacher's methods.

Another way of finding a teacher is to observe the kind of student the teacher produces. However, if the beginner is less interested in developing a skill than in inner development, this method also has drawbacks. How do we determine a person's inner development? If a student attending a school we are investigating appears to have attained some measure of maturity, how do we know that it is the result of the training he does and was not already present in him when he began his training? Perhaps the beginner will look to the ranking system used in many martial arts in the hope that it will serve as a criterion for judging the development of students. He would then expect students with higher ranks to demonstrate a greater degree of the kind of growth he seeks. Unfortunately, martial arts ranking systems seldom represent more than a relative placement based on the attainment of skill and of the required amount of time in the rank below.

A way around these problems is to base the selection of a teacher on his reputation. Martial arts are widely enough practiced so that our acquaintances will include a few persons who have some knowledge about the field. They might know which teachers are suitable for the beginner's needs. If their knowledge of the field fails to extend to these lengths, they may know of someone engaged in the study of martial arts who might have the required information. In this way, the beginner may be able to find the kind of teacher he is looking for.

The suggested methods of finding the right teacher should help the beginner in his search. However, still other factors appear to be involved in this situation. My observation over the years as a student and teacher of various martial arts is that the theory held in many esoteric circles, that "like attracts like," is valid. Beginners seem to gravitate to a teacher who reflects or shares or harmonizes with their inner evolution. The teacher may be perceived, often almost unconsciously, as being well along on the path the beginner himself has embarked on or is drawn to.

This process of selecting a teacher is usually not as clear-cut as it is described, if indeed the description was clear-cut. A person may begin studying with a teacher he has decided is right for him only to find, after a few months, that he was mistaken. Where this occurs, the student involved often has not been enrolled long enough to make such a decision. He should stay at the school of his choice for at least two years before he determines that the kind of training given there is not what he wants. If he has been careful in his choice at the outset and if he is serious about training, he will have lost nothing by withdrawing after he has given the particular school a fair chance.

Choosing the right teacher, then, is clearly an important step for a beginner. But after he has made his choice, he is soon confronted with the impediments to understanding mentioned above. How should he proceed? If he can, a beginner should come to his training without preconceptions about what he is going to learn. This is probably impossible, because the fact of his enrolling in a school means that he has given some thought to martial arts and, naturally, expects something from his study. He probably has read or heard of the benefits such training bestows on its practitioners and thinks he has a good idea of what these benefits are. Thus, many students appear for instruction believing they know what they are going to learn, expecting the teacher to proceed in a certain way and looking for quick changes in themselves. When the teacher does not behave as they think he should or when the kind of development they envisioned fails to manifest itself quickly enough, they are disappointed and often stop practicing. They have led themselves into a disappointing situation because they failed to see that their expectation, or intellectualization, is not the real thing.

Of course, the real thing may not be what they want anyway, but it is only after experiencing the reality of it as clearly as possible that they can make a decision about it. Moreover, this kind of experiencing must take place over the span of a few years. In that period of time, the potentials the training encompasses ought to reveal themselves. In addition, the student will know more clearly what is meant by some of the statements he thought he understood when he started out. It is most productive for the student to practice with a mind that is to the fullest possible extent, open, attentive and aware. Conceptions about what is being taught and learned that come from a source other than practice usually get in the way of the direct experience. The ideas that come from this direct experience are the only ones the student really understands and even these are subject to change as practice continues.

CHAPTER VII

Summary and Conclusion

THE PREVIOUS chapters have attempted to examine the mental and physical changes experienced by students who undertake a serious study of martial arts with a competent teacher. In summary, such training affects students in the following ways:

Most apparent and easily visible are the results of the physical exercise encountered in training. Pursuing a regimen of regular physical exercise helps promote better physical and mental health. We might find that we are seldom ill and that we have sufficient energy to do our day's work without becoming overly tired. Certainly, we become physically stronger and our body attains, or retains, a youthful look in which the muscles are firm and excess fat is absent. This exercise also serves as a harmless outlet for frustration and helps to relieve the damaging physical and mental effects of the stress of modern life.

Equally visible, but requiring a longer period of time to appear, is the learning of a skill. We become able to use our body effectively in attack and defense. Our movements grow more efficient and we learn to conserve energy. Also, we become aware that we must subject ourselves to discipline if we are to practice diligently enough to attain the skill we seek. The external form of discipline characterisitic of martial arts training gradually becomes internalized as we realize that in order to become accomplished in anything we must persevere in our practice over some years.

Because relatively few persons in our society have spent a few years in a serious study of martial arts and gained the skill that comes with such dedication, it is the sort of accomplishment that contributes to a feeling of personal worth. That is, even if we have not gone very far or achieved much in other areas of life, we have proved to ourselves that we have the energy, discipline and whatever else is required to do something worthwhile with some measure of distinction. We begin to feel that we are all right.

On another level, the growth of self-understanding and an increased knowledge of others are promoted by martial arts training. These capacities should develop in all of us as we grow older and gain experience in living. However, training of the sort encountered in martial arts is designed to enhance the growth of these qualities. Nevertheless, it is somewhat difficult to measure and assess the nature of this growth because it develops slowly and is, beyond question, affected by the lives we lead outside the training hall.

We also become aware of the value of employing a more intuitive way of relating to life than has been the custom in our society. Aspects of our training are designed to encourage the growth and use of this faculty by relaxing or giving reduced play to the logical, analytical portion of the mind. Logical reasoning and analysis is not negated but is given the appropriate and indispensable task of weighing, measuring, ordering and making coherent the world we are part of. However, this capacity is not permitted to occupy the whole field to the extent that we ignore or are frightened or suspicious of information about ourselves or others that comes from other levels or areas of the mind.

Finally, we become able, with varying degrees of success, to focus our mind on each passing moment. We learn to act without thinking of where we have been or where we are going. Thoughts of past and future are usually irrelevant and will inhibit action. If our mind strays from complete attention to the matter at hand, our position grows weaker. Moreover, conscious or analytical thoughts at such times block or distort the freshness of the moment. We no longer really see what is happening, but are busy comparing and analyzing.

The gradual outcome of such training might be said to be the growth of maturity. The physical and mental settling that occurs gives us a calm approach to the exigencies of daily life, a bearing that is not easily upset. We are to a lesser extent than most caught up in the sometimes frantic pace

132

characteristic of modern life. But where quick action is appropriate and necessary, we find ourselves adequate to the emergency. As we go as quietly as possible about our daily round, we find ourselves more awake in the sense of seeing ourselves and others with additional clarity. We become increasingly alert to what we are doing and what is going on around us. Conducting ourselves in this way stems from an inner strength or mental state which martial arts training has planted and helped nurture.

Having heard of these desirable outcomes, and often misinterpreting their nature, people will come to the martial arts with rather extravagant expectations about what training will do for them. However, most will not view their study as an end in itself but as a help in improving other aspects of their lives. Those who have determined their objectives in life often intend to make use of this training to help them progress more rapidly toward achieving their goals. In our society, these goals are usually concerned with getting some kind of work that is secure and capable of providing a good salary. The emphasis is often on getting ahead in the sense of moving to a job that pays more money than one previously held. Of course, money is seldom the only reason a person gets and holds a job. Many workers are interested in what they are doing beyond the urge for security and money. They may feel that the work they do helps others or is interesting or worthwhile for other reasons. Moreover, industrial firms that employ assembly line techniques have of late been concerned with lower productivity caused by worker boredom. They found that even a fairly good wage fails to compensate sufficiently for an uninteresting or overly repetitive job. Yet if it comes to a question of status or relative position in life, we usually judge achievement by the amount of money a man earns or has amassed and how he spends it. It is not that we desire money for its own sake. Rather, we believe that with money we can buy things, as well as gain freedom, power and the respect of others. It is reasoned by those who think they have insufficient money, a group which comprises the great majority, that gaining what money can buy will bring contentment and happiness.

Better health, more self-confidence, increased energy and a feeling of calmness might then be considered excellent equipment for use in the drive to achieve the goals toward which people in our society generally strive. This view, in a limited sense, is unarguable. But we must consider an additional factor. This concerns the tremendous psychological pressure on workers by jobs which pay well or positions which are desirable. The mental stress of modern life affects all of us whether our economic level is high or low. But especially heavy demands are made on those who compete for more attractive positions. Some, possessing a fortuitous combination of innate equipment, such as high intelligence, mental stability, and a strong constitution, can meet these pressures with seeming success. They are able to assume very demanding positions and appear to thrive there. However, we need only look about us to notice the many who must resort to tranquilizers or alcohol for relief from pressure. Others, under more mental strain than they can handle, neglect their health and succumb at far too early an age to heart disease or some other ailment.

Naturally, we all have the ability to deal with a certain amount of stress without suffering unduly. Sometimes we even welcome the appearance of a little something out of the ordinary that makes us call upon seldom used internal resources. Living might be said to consist of seeking the solution to problems we set ourselves. The search for such solutions always produces some degree of mental strain. Within certain limits such strain is normal and healthy. But if the pressures prove too great and we become ill, we may be learning that this way of living is not for us. Moreover, if certain of our objectives prove empty or unrewarding when they are reached, we may again know through our experience that what we seek may lie elsewhere.

If such suspicions about the way we are living begin to surface, we might then question our use of the ability, gained through martial arts training, to work in a stronger, more focused, way. We may give up the attempt to labor longer hours or more efficiently at an irritating or exasperating job in order to secure an ever-higher level of material wealth. If our scramble for material success produces unhealthy amounts of tension and stress, expending more energy in that direction appears self-defeating. The pattern could continue with any gain in additional serenity, calmness and available energy being offset by greater exposure, in terms of intensity or length of time, to an unhealthy situation.

The necessities for preserving life are presently rather easily secured in today's industrialized societies. But most of us are not concerned with merely earning enough money to provide food and shelter. We are made to feel by the advertising of corporations with products to sell that a minimum kind of food and shelter are insufficient. This commercial message is reinforced or even outdone by the expectations of family and friends concerning the attainment or maintenance of a particular living standard. We are told implicitly that our happiness depends on having more things or things of better quality that cost more. Perhaps the relative material prosperity of our economic system depends upon the generation of this kind of demand, but that is a long question. The suspicion grows, however, especially among the young, that the drive for, or the success in, accumulating money or material things does not necessarily bring happiness or contentment. In addition, some people realize that the search for the attainment of such abstractions as personal freedom, power and the respect of others may have little to do with the accumulation of material wealth.

Others, especially those able to see themselves with some measure of clarity, may notice that the purchase of some additional thing fails to bring the happiness or contentment they imagined. There may be some initial satisfaction, but this feeling is soon forgotten as the overriding concern with getting more crowds in. This condition of mind does not seem to change merely through the accumulation of additional material wealth. It must be altered in some other way.

What seems necessary is a reassessment of what is worthwhile in life. Moreover, we must give some thought to the means used to attain our objectives. Perhaps the price we must pay for material plenty is too high in terms of mental and physical stress and resultant deterioration. Perhaps the security we seek does not lie in this area. But to attempt such a reassessment through the use of logic and even to make a decision to change our approach is only the first step. It must be reinforced, if a real and permanent change is to result, by the full range of our mental and emotional faculties. Also, this work must proceed over the months and years, especially if the environment in which such change is to take place is unfavorable.

Those whose thinking runs in this vein can find such reinforcement through the study of martial arts under a competent teacher. But even if our conscious thoughts have not gone in the direction described above, beyond perhaps a vague unease with the progress of events in our world, when we embark seriously on the kind of training described we begin to experience a slow change in our outlook on life. For example, we may begin to sense in ourselves an attraction to those age-old prescriptions for living that relegate the accumulation of material wealth to a less prominent position than that generally found in our society. We may find working on ourselves rewarding in many ways, and that accomplishment of this kind need not be measured by the yardstick of material gain. Placing such work in a paramount position in the conduct of life seems to be the advice of the wisest minds of the past.

An outlook on life that is not overly dependent for contentment on material plenty may well be especially appropriate in the coming decades. Without being unduly pessimistic about the course of future events in this country and in the world, the view appears less than bright. We are faced with an ever increasing number of people in the world. Quite possibly we will be unable to find solutions to the problems connected with feeding and providing other basic necessities for the projected population expansion. Certainly such a possibility must be considered with some degree of alarm.

Those who live in the industrialized countries of the world may feel that the concerns of less fortunate areas, where the problems of feeding a rapidly expanding population are especially acute, need not worry them. However, aside from humanitarian considerations for the plight of these people, indications are that the living standard of persons in developed areas will not continue to rise as in the past. It is doubtful if this standard will even continue at the same level. Because the earth contains a limited amount of the raw materials that industrialized countries need for their continued growth and prosperity, it seems fairly clear that we cannot continue to use them at the same rate as in the past. As the supply diminishes, the various components from which manufactured products are made will become increasingly expensive. This situation cannot but effect a decline in the rate of industrial growth. It appears that the idea of industrial growth, of turning out an ever greater volume of goods, must give way to an emphasis on the husbanding of resources. We will be forced to stop using what we have as though our supplies were unlimited. Also, it might be to our advantage, or even necessary, to view man's place in the world in a different way from that typical of our past. We are coming to realize that we are more closely tied to the earth and that our options are more limited in scope than our past thinking has led us to believe.

To ask that we in the West alter our thinking about Nature from an emphasis on manipulation to an attempt at achieving greater harmony is probably unrealistic. The attitudes and the approach to life developed over a few thousand years in the West seem to move us in certain directions and elicit particular responses to problems which elsewhere might be handled differently. Our Western response to the threat of decreasing natural resources and an insufficient food supply for an expanding population will most likely continue to be one of manipulation. Through the use of additional technology, we will try to increase our food output, reduce population growth and look for ways to make goods that conserve scarce raw materials. Yet, there is little question that we in the West, and people throughout the world, are faced with tremendous problems. We have certainly become overextended in the exploitation of limited resources. The balance must be righted if we wish to avoid disaster.

Despite the prevailing attitude of the West concerning man's role in the world, thinking does change over time. In all likelihood, however, it will not be the force or attraction of a new idea but necessity which will cause us in the West to take a more respectful view of Nature. As the world begins to run short of food and raw material, we may come to realize that our survival may be at stake and that unusual measures are called for.

We may have personally felt or heard others express revulsion for the course of Western thinking which gave rise to scientific inquiry and which is partly responsible for our ability to destroy ourselves and much of the rest of life. Many of the problems the world faces today are often traced to the practical outcome of this Western attraction to finding out what makes things go. But such feelings should not cause us to close our eyes to the many achievements in greatly increased understanding of ourselves and our world made through scientific endeavor. This knowledge, properly used, can contribute immeasurably to the welfare of mankind. It is highly doubtful, moreover, that were another culture dominant in the world we would be better off than we are presently. We may feel that the philosophical and religious speculation about man and Nature characteristic of some cultures represents reality more closely than past or present Western thinking. We could take the view that the world would be in a better state if such ideas held sway. However, if we examine the history of other cultures we cannot help but notice that the practical course of events was not always in keeping with some of the humanitarian ideas expounded by philosophers. Those who ruled were frequently unmindful of the welfare of their subjects. In addition, these societies were so subject to the capriciousness of Nature that famine and pestilence periodically deprived countless numbers of their lives.

To summarize, the opportunity for many of us to achieve material plenty on the level we know it in the West seems to be accompanied by the use of the world's limited natural resources at a rate that cannot continue. If we share the predominant view of life in American society, most of us are probably going to be disappointed as previous levels of affluence become increasingly difficult to achieve. Our thinking and attitudes about what constitutes the good life will have to change. Unfortunately, no one can predict with any degree of certainty the course our lives are going to take. All kinds of solutions to our problems have been offered and will be attempted. Mankind seems never to have been free of problems of varying magnitude. But in every age, the qualities of mind and body gained from a study of martial arts would have stood an individual in good stead.

A final word. Most of us seem to be searching for some kind of solid base in ourselves, a secure position that will stand fast and not crumble when assailed by the various ills that human beings have to endure. This search is reflected in the feeling that we lack something. We think that we will become the mature, content and attractive kind of person we envision if only we could add some element to ourselves. This imagined addition might be a certain amount of money or some material object, like our own home. Because many of us believe our personal security depends heavily on the satisfaction of material needs or desires, this final chapter has explored, to a limited extent, the part played in our lives by economic considerations. But the addition need not be monetary or material. It might be a change in our appearance, the love or possession of another person or the fruit of some kind of study or training.

However, we must come to realize that we are all right just as we are. If we fail to move beyond the illusion that adding something to what we are will make us whole, we will be engaged in an endless search. We will find that the acquisition of the hoped for object or attribute has failed to change us in the way we thought it would. Our search then continues. We are unaware that we were and are complete without adding or changing anything.

If we recognize this, life does not necessarily become easier. We may still engage in the various activities we enjoy or that interest us. But we do approach what we do in a different way. We no longer waste our physical and mental energies searching for something we had all the time. We can devote ourselves to living from day to day, to solving our problems as they arise, in the knowledge that whatever the outcome, we are engaged in an exciting and joyous activity—being alive.

Why then study martial arts? Aside from having elements that can enhance the quality of our life, this form of training can bring us to a sense of our wholeness. This sense or realization will probably begin as an intellectualization. Internalizing this idea, making it a part of ourselves, takes time and needs work. The realization, once it appears, is like a small seedling that must be nurtured until it grows strong in us. Continued training provides the reinforcement necessary for the proper growth of this valuable plant.